High Wood

High Wood

Michael Harrison

Pen & Sword
MILITARY

First published in Great Britain in 2017 by
PEN AND SWORD MILITARY
an imprint of
Pen and Sword Books Ltd
47 Church Street
Barnsley
South Yorkshire S70 2AS

ISBN 978 1 47383 409 5

Printed and bound in England by
CPI Group (UK) Ltd, Croydon, CR0 4YY

Typeset in Times New Roman by CHIC GRAPHICS

Pen & Sword Books Ltd incorporates the imprints of
Pen & Sword Books Ltd incorporates the imprints of Pen & Sword
Archaeology, Atlas, Aviation, Battleground, Discovery,
Family History, History, Maritime, Military, Naval, Politics,
Railways, Select, Social History, Transport, True Crime,
Claymore Press, Frontline Books, Leo Cooper, Praetorian Press,
Remember When, Seaforth Publishing and Wharncliffe.

For a complete list of Pen and Sword titles please contact
Pen and Sword Books Limited
47 Church Street, Barnsley, South Yorkshire, S70 2AS, England
E-mail: enquiries@pen-and-sword.co.uk
Website: www.pen-and-sword.co.uk

Contents

Acknowledgements

My sincere thanks to all those mentioned below as without their unstinting help and encouragement this book would never have seen the light of day.

Lee Harrison, whose idea for the book followed a dusty walk over the Somme Battlefield to High Wood.

Terry Carter (author of *Birmingham Pals*) for use of his research material relating to High Wood and his particular skills in locating features in the landscape around it.

Lynette and Mark Bentley for their skills and patience in proof reading, computing and, in particular, when the part-finished document was 'lost'.

Tim Pierce and colleagues of Royal Air Force Cranwell College Hall Library, for their expertise and encouragement.

Rex and Lynn Gregson for the unlimited and long-term use of their extensive library and unfailing support.

Dr Spencer Jones, of the University of Wolverhampton, with his vast knowledge of the First World War and his willingness to allot time to a former student.

Professor Gary Sheffield, who spared time and expertise for a former student.

John Hamblin, of Lancing College in Sussex, for his permission to use material relating to Captain Harold Webb.

Charles Fair, for his permission (originally granted to Terry Carter) to use archive material relating to Major Charles Fair.

Major John Pratt, a true soldier, never downhearted and who can 'read the war' from a map like no other.

Doctor Christopher Pugsley, author of *Haig and the Implementation of Tactical Doctrine on the Western Front.* Irene Moore for her editing, guidance and supreme patience.

Finally, the person who drove this project in all its aspects: Mrs Joyce Harrison who never once baulked at any set back on the road to completion and pushed harder still when resolve might have flagged, and all without instituting divorce proceedings.

Introduction

High Wood
14 July – 15 September 1916

Bois de Fourcaux (Pitchfork Wood) was known to the British Army on the Somme as High Wood, a name that has reverberated down the decades for its sinister reputation as the scene of some of the fiercest fighting in the British sector of the Anglo-French offensive of 1916. This series of actions undertaken over a period of approximately five months is now known to history as the Battle of the Somme. High Wood covers an area of 75 acres (a tiny fraction of the 120 square miles of the Somme battlefield) and stands brooding atop a rise 500ft above sea level in the undulating landscape of the Somme battlefield. All is peaceful now, but the long ago summer of the year 1916 witnessed a titanic struggle that took place when the soldiers of the British Expeditionary Force (BEF) crashed into those of Germany in the struggle for possession of High Wood.

High Wood has previously been the subject of various works in books and articles including *The Hell They Called High Wood*, a seminal work by the late Terry Norman which certainly repays the time of the reader. However, the kernel for our work came about when two members of a small party, Lee Harrison and Terry Carter, elected to walk from Bazentin-le-Grand to High Wood via the routes used by many of the attacking British troops in July 1916. Upon their eventual arrival at High Wood, dusty, bedraggled and thirsty, both walkers commented that they became ever more conscious of being under observation from the wood as they slogged across the rolling downland that had separated the British front lines from High Wood.

Following discussion, it was concluded that in the hands of a competent hostile army, High Wood was a killing machine; a machine that had to be neutralised before there could be any chance of success for the British in this sector of the Somme battlefield. With mounting levels of interest concerning Great Britain's role in the First World War, and in particular the fighting on the Somme, Pen and Sword concluded that a book detailing the colossal effort made by the British Army to wrest control of the wood from its German occupiers would be both useful and informative to the battlefield visitor and also for those whose circumstances prevent them from travelling to this now quiet backwater of rural France. Here High Wood stands a lonely sentinel, keeping an eternal vigil over a landscape that witnessed scenes almost beyond comprehension or description.

Because of space limitations it will not be possible to describe the minutiae of two months of struggle for High Wood, due mainly to the complexity of wood fighting and the sheer number of battalions that took part. Dr G. Payne, in a 2008 article for the Western Front Association, calculated that sixty-four battalions, from forty-seven different regiments took part in the attacks on High Wood. For this reason the work has been divided into five chapters covering significant dates in the fighting for the wood during July, August and September 1916. Important and separate mining attacks that took place at High Wood are also included in the narrative.

The British Army was not on the Somme by accident or whim. Britain was allied to France and Belgium, both of whom had been invaded by Germany whose government proclaimed that the territory so gained was now German. The front lines facing west now constituted the German frontier, with the added intention to drive to the Channel and North Sea coastlines from where Britain's trade and food lifelines would be disrupted and/or severed. Apart from appeasement, Great Britain together with France and Belgium had no other option but to expel the invader. It is neither our wish nor intention to re-open old sores, but unless history is truthful it is worthless.

The Greek historian, Polybius, who was born circa 203BC, defined history thus:

> *If you take the truth from History what is left is but an idle unprofitable tale. Therefore, one must not shrink either from blaming one's friends or praising one's enemies: or be afraid of finding fault with and commending the same persons at different times. For it is impossible that men engaged in public affairs*

should always be right, and unlikely that they should always be wrong. Holding ourselves, therefore entirely aloof from the actors, we must as historians make statements and pronounce judgements in accordance with the actions themselves.

In this work we shall endeavour to abide by the advice of Polybius, however the 'truth' can be a very elusive species. As there is now no longer anyone living who fought at High Wood, historians have no choice but to rely largely on written records; in doing so, it should be borne in mind that it is human nature not to indulge in self criticism when preparing documents to be read by higher authority, or indeed posterity. The same caution should be exercised when reading post First World War publications produced by people who took a direct part in events, or were members of political establishments; anything that went wrong was always someone else's fault and usually the writer could and would have done much better if only he had been in command of events.

Following careful consideration, archive material is used in the text together with published sources that have been subjected to the same criteria. Archaeological and physical study of High Wood is not possible at the time of writing. The wood is private property and, coupled with ever more complex legislation and the rising costs involved with battlefield archaeology, it seems that for the foreseeable future High Wood and the physical remains of the fighting therein, will continue to be an enigma.

High Wood – closed to visitors.

Time as expressed in written and verbal forms

All references to hours of the day or night are as used by the British Army during the First World War. The twenty-four hour clock was not in widespread use, a.m. (ack emma) or p.m. (pip emma), being the standard in written orders, ack emma and pip emma being used to transmit speech in what was known as 'signalese'.

British Army map references and spot heights

The map references contained within the text are of the standard type used by the British Expeditionary Force (BEF) during the First World War, distance being expressed in yards; the spot heights are as French maps of the time and expressed in metres. The grid lines run north to south and east to west. The maps are divided into sections denoted by a capital letter, which in turn are broken down into numbered squares of 1000 x 1000 yards, and further reduced to sub squares 500 x 500 yards denoted by a, b, c and d, 50 x 50 yards. By sub dividing again, a square of 5 x 5 yards can be plotted. Most of the references used in this work are covered by map Longueval, 2.E 15-8 1916. Read off the sub square letter and number west to east to obtain eastings, followed by the second south to north to give northings; where the lines converge is the position denoted by the reference.

British Army Formations and Units

For clarity and ease of reading, here follows a brief explanation regarding the basic organisation of the BEF operating in France and Flanders for most of 1916. **Formations** denoted organisations from brigade upwards. **Units** denoted all organisations below brigades.

Commander in Chief: General Sir Douglas Haig (promoted Field Marshal, 27 December 1916).

Army: a semi-permanent formation, Great Britain would eventually operate five armies on the Western Front. The battles for High Wood were mainly conducted by Fourth Army, commanded by General Sir Henry Rawlinson, with some units of the Reserve Army.

Corps: these were also semi permanent formations directly responsible to the army commander and containing two or more divisions. A corps was usually commanded by a lieutenant general.

Division: this was a permanent formation, usually commanded by a major general, comprising an all-arms formation, including artillery. At full strength, a division would number some 19,372 officers and other ranks, of whom at best, 12,000 would be infantry.

Brigades: were usually commanded by a brigadier general, each division was divided into three infantry brigades; in 1916 each brigade consisted of four battalions of infantry.

Battalions: usually commanded by a lieutenant colonel. Figures vary as to the full strength of a battalion from 959-1007, though units were rarely at full strength, especially as the Somme campaign progressed.

The Company: the battalions of 1916 officially contained four companies of 217 officers and other ranks, each company being commanded by a major or a captain.

The Platoon: officially made up of fifty-two men, each platoon being commanded by a lieutenant or second lieutenant.

The Section: made up of at least one (quite often two) non commissioned officer and twelve private soldiers.

The map below, reproduced by Terry Carter from a newspaper article published in October 1916, illustrates the dominant position of High Wood on the Somme battlefield.

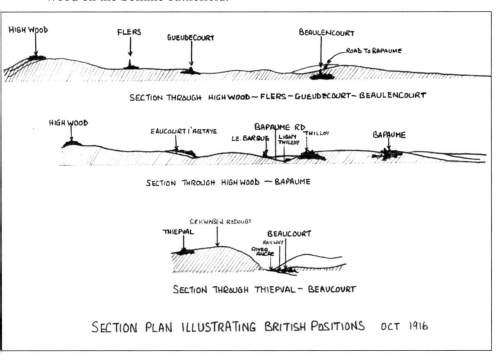

SECTION THROUGH HIGH WOOD – FLERS – GUEUDECOURT – BEAULENCOURT

SECTION THROUGH HIGH WOOD – BAPAUME

SECTION THROUGH THIEPVAL – BEAUCOURT

SECTION PLAN ILLUSTRATING BRITISH POSITIONS   OCT 1916

Timeline

The Actions Leading to the Final Capture of High Wood

1 July 1916: The capture of Montauban by 30th Division, XIII Corps, Fourth Army.

10 July: Capture of Contalmaison by 23rd Division, III Corps, Fourth Army.

11 July: Capture of Mametz Wood by 38th (Welsh) Division, XV Corps, Fourth Army.

14 July: Capture of Trônes Wood by 54 Brigade, 18th (Eastern) Division, XIII Corps, Fourth Army.
Battle of Bazentin Ridge: III Corps, XIII Corps, XV Corps, Fourth Army and X Corps, Reserve Army.

20–30 July: Attacks against High Wood by 19th (Western) Division, Reserve Army, III Corps, 5th, 7th, 33rd and 51st (Highland) Division, XV Corps.

27 July: Partial capture of Delville Wood by 2nd Division, XIII Corps, Fourth Army.

28 July: Line of Duke Street (Delville Wood) reached by 5th Division, XV Corps, Fourth Army.

18 August: 33rd Division make an unsuccessful attack on Wood Lane but elements of 1st Division enter the Switch Line unopposed.

24 August: Large scale co-ordinated attack launched by Fourth Army against High Wood and Delville Wood.

25 August: Delville Wood reported clear of German troops – British making small gains in High Wood.

3 September: British mine exploded in High Wood – 2nd Royal Welch Fusiliers reach the centre of High Wood.

8 September: III Corps deploy 1st Division to attack western part of High Wood – some success but troops withdrawn.

15 September: High Wood falls to 47th (London) Division flanked by 50th (Northumbrian) and New Zealand Division.

Chapter 1

The Dawn Attack:
'They dared, they have managed.'

Friday 14 July, 70°F. Overcast.

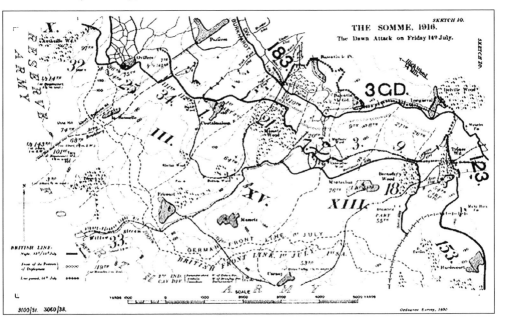

The map, reproduced from the *British Official History*, depicts Fourth Army's gains on 14 July 1916. Interestingly, High Wood is not shown but referred to by an arrow pointing north-west from Delville Wood.

List of British Army formations involved in, or acting as 'flank guards' during the dawn attack:

Army: Fourth Army (General Sir H.S. Rawlinson)
Corps: III Corps (Lieutenant General W.P. Pulteney), XIII Corps (Lieutenant General W.N. Congreve VC), XV Corps (Lieutenant General H.S. Horne)

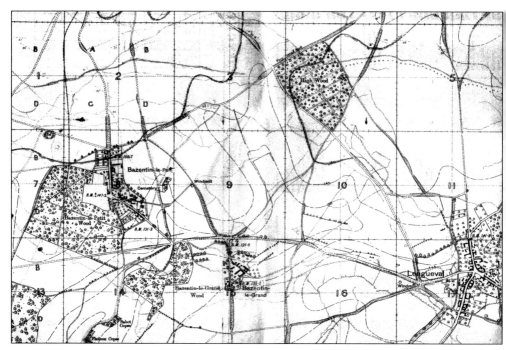

High Wood and its environs, 1916 – note the contour lines, they are very important in the understanding of the battles for High Wood.

Divisions: 1st, 3rd, 7th, 9th (Scottish), 18th (Eastern), 21st, 33rd, 34th, 35th (Bantam)

The visitor to High Wood would be entitled to ask the question, why here? What was so important about this particular wood, it is after all only one of many to be found on the former battlefield? The answer lies in the name applied to the wood by the British. High Wood dominates the landscape in all directions and in 1916 possession of the wood allowed the British observation over the enemy's third battle line and much of the country east of it, including the elusive first day objective of Bapaume. Artillery was 'queen of the battlefield' during the First World War and direct observation was paramount, without which the ever-growing power of the Royal Artillery could not be brought to bear. To be successful in the application of their art, the gunners needed to be sure of two fixed points (a) where the shell begins its journey and (b) where it actually lands as opposed to the intended destination. Aerial observation would also play an increasingly important role for the gunners as communication techniques improved to the point that German troops came to dread the appearance of a British 'spotter' aircraft, as they knew full well that a hurricane of flying steel would soon be on its way to them. But 'eyes on' observation, which also included the use of captive balloons, would remain of the highest importance to both sides throughout the First World War.

The two months of fighting for possession of High Wood was punctuated by cavalry and mining attacks, massive artillery duels, the use of the new tank and, of mammoth importance, large loss of life for attacking and defending infantry.

Just under two weeks had passed since the disastrous British attack of 1 July, yet Fourth Army was re-equipped, had new formations and, with a much shorter front, had a higher concentration of field artillery and howitzers per mile than on that day. Fourth Army was going to attack the enemy's Second Line, on a 6,000 yard front located upon the Bazentin Ridge, in the early hours of 14 July with two corps, fielding five divisions and employing 22,000 troops. The French had serious misgivings regarding a night attack by troops who, in their professional opinion, were not fully trained for the work and thus only disaster could ensue. In reality the French had a point, the BEF, for all its expanding numbers and growing abundance in equipment, had very little experience of conducting massive operations and, worryingly, still suffered from defective artillery ammunition and partly-trained gunners.

A new version of the forest giant: Mammoth French howitzer articulates the will of France.

The local French corps commander, General Balfourier, expressed his concerns via his liaison officer to Major General A.A. Montgomery, Rawlinson's chief of staff, Fourth Army on 13 July. Montgomery replied:

> *Tell General Balfourier, with my compliments, that if we are not on the Longueval Ridge at eight tomorrow morning I will eat my hat.*

The power of artillery cannot be underestimated; it was no idle boast by King Louis XIV of France (the 'Sun King', 1638-1715) that artillery was *Ultima Ratio Regum*, which has been translated as 'the final argument of kings'. These expensive and highly destructive machines dictated the outcome of many wars and the First World War was no exception. On this day Fourth Army was supported by some 1,000 guns, including 311 howitzers and heavy pieces, a firepower concentration five times greater than that available for the 1 July assault. In effect, one heavy howitzer was deployed for every 19 yards of front and one 18-pdr field gun every 6 yards.

Extra protection for the attacking infantry came in the form of a creeping barrage and the use of time fuses as opposed to the widely used 'No.100 graze' fuse, which could cause the shell to detonate by brushing a tree branch or telephone wire. It was feared that troops who were 'leaning on' the creeping barrage could be killed or wounded by friendly fire. In contrast to graze fuses, which were more liable to premature bursting, the time delay type would detonate one-tenth of a second after contact with the target.

In order for the attack planned for 14 July (the Battle of Bazentin Ridge) to succeed, the left and right flanks of the attacking formations had to be secured. This entailed taking Mametz Wood on the left flank and Trônes Wood on the right. Mametz Wood was secured by 12 July following heroic efforts by the 38th (Welsh) Division (Major General G.C. Blackader) and 21st Division (Major General D.G.M. Campbell. Trônes Wood on the right flank did not actually fall to the 18th Division (Major General F.I. Maxse) until 9.30am on 14 July.

By 2.30am on that day, the attacking troops of XIII and XV Corps, comprising eighteen separate infantry brigades, were assembled in their jumping-off positions, with advanced troops having left their trenches and taken up positions in complete silence within 300-500 yards of the enemy. At 3.20am the Royal Artillery opened a 'hurricane' bombardment of the German positions with French artillery lending support on the right flank. Writing in the *Official History*, Brigadier General Sir J.E. Edmonds described the bombardment:

> *The whole sky behind the waiting infantry of the four attacking divisions seemed to open with a great roar. For five minutes the ground in front was alive with bursting shell, whilst the machine guns, firing on lines laid before dark on the previous evening, pumped streams of bullets to clear the way.*

The effect of this concentrated firepower upon the German defenders can be summarised by the recollections of a German officer, quoted by Christopher Duffy in *Through German Eyes*:

> *We heard a snarling and hissing in the air, and in a matter of seconds the whole landscape to front and rear as well as our own positions were enveloped in smoke, dust, and fumes. It was a furious and mighty fire which made the terrors of Notre Dame de Lorette seem almost like child's play.*

This illustrates the rapid evolution of the tactics of the Royal Artillery; just a fortnight previously the gunners had been unable to destroy the enemy's barbed wire. The wide frontage of the 1 July attack and the multiplicity of tasks assigned to the guns, plus the 30 per cent of shells which had failed to explode, had seriously thinned out the effects of the bombardment. The gunners' tasks had included: destruction of the enemy's wire and trenches; suppression of his field and heavy gun batteries; disruption of all his known transport routes; destruction of all known enemy assembly points, ammunition and supply dumps and destruction of his command system. It was just too heavy a workload for the men and the guns to fulfil successfully and it robbed the infantry of the protection that should have been afforded them on 1 July.

Jack Sheldon in *The German Army on the Somme* quotes Reserve Leutnant Borelli of the German 77th Reserve Regiment's 106th Machine Gun Company who, on 14 July, discovered that they were full in the path of the attack launched by the British 21st Division:

The enemy assaulted in about six waves, these were not dressed lines of infantry; rather they were concentrated groups of soldiers. My machine gun crews suffered heavy casualties because the British, who were sheltering in the craters directly to our front, could not be brought under fire and so were able to throw grenades with impunity in to the area of the machine guns.

By 1pm Fourth Army had achieved a remarkable surprise victory with most objectives on the Bazentin Ridge attained, largely with the least experienced troops of Kitchener's 'New Army'. High Wood was in plain sight from the Bazentin-le-Petit to Longueval road and all seemed quiet in no man's land.

Two exceptions to Fourth Army's success comprised the northern corner of Bazentin-le-Petit Wood and the fortified village of Longueval. In the case of Longueval, a series of conflicting reports concerning the whole, partial, or non-occupation of the village effectively blinded the higher staffs. Without the fully assured clearance of the two locations mentioned above, Fourth Army commanders deemed that any moves against High Wood would be caught in open ground by enfilade fire as in the jaws of a trap, a case of 'fog of war' which blinds commanders and gives rise to inertia. The 'fog' evolves from the breakdown of communications and intelligence that quickly becomes out of date following first contact with the enemy and is a constant throughout military history. Due to re-occurring breakages in the field telephone lines, reports had to be sent back to senior commanders by the use of runners. These very brave men often took hours to reach their assigned destination, by which time the intelligence they had risked their lives to deliver could be out of date or, if the runner was unfortunate enough to be killed or wounded during his journey, then the message would not get through at all. The same could happen in reverse, a commander could 'peer into the fog' and make a decision based on the intelligence available to him. Providing his runner survived the journey to the front lines and the recipient had not been killed, wounded, or gone to ground in a maze of trenches and shell holes, the message could get through and possibly influence the outcome of the battle.

The fog of war was not a product of the First World War, the great Chinese military thinker Sun Tzu, writing in the fourth century BC, expounded on the need for reliable intelligence. In the nineteenth century, the author of *On War*, Carl von Clausewitz wrote that 'friction' (fog) bedevils all military actions. As recently as 2001, the American military author Edwin Luttwak defined military operations thus:

> *The race for intelligence (reliable and up to date), the race to manoeuvre, the race to chaos; the protagonist who re-sets the race at the point of chaos before his opponent can react is more likely to be victorious.*

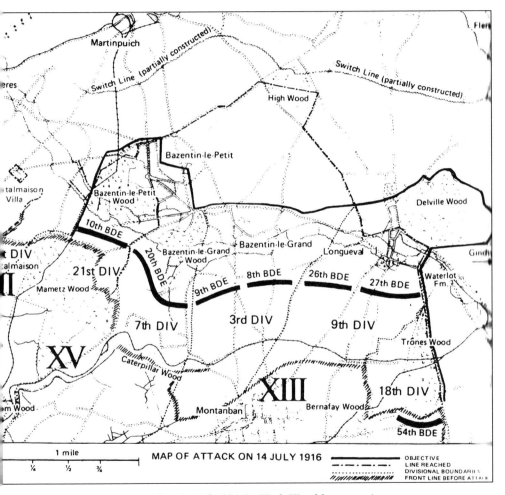

Battle of Bazentin Ridge, 14 July 1916 – High Wood lay empty)

Incredibly, High Wood had been abandoned by the enemy early on 14 July and as proof at least three senior British officers walked across no man's land to High Wood and returned safely without a shot being fired. In a letter to the official historian and quoted by Terry Norman, the commanding officer of 9 Brigade, Brigadier General H.C. Potter, wrote:

> *I walked out alone to examine the ground in front. It was a lovely day; the ground was very open and slopped gently up to a high ridge in front, so I wandered on until I found myself approaching a large wood which continued over the crest of a ridge. There was no sign whatever of the enemy, so I walked into the edge of the wood, but saw no sign of a German, nor any defensive works. As I had advanced about a mile, and was quite alone, I considered it time to return, the wood reached by me I afterwards knew as High Wood.*

Brigadier General Potter further related that it was a source of great regret to him that the wood had not been taken when there had been a real opportunity to do so. The two other officers who walked to High Wood separately from Brigadier General Potter, were Lieutenant Colonel C.A. Elliot of the Royal Engineers, who was accompanied by another engineer officer named Playfair, who was also of the firm opinion that High Wood 'could have been occupied straight away'. The above reports should not be treated as hindsight, as these men actually walked safely to High Wood and at least one officer entered the wood, ironically achieving something that the battlefield visitor of today cannot do.

Fourth Army was poised to strike, but failed to do so decisively, allowing the ever resourceful Germans, aided by their partially completed Switch Line (known to them as *Foureaux Riegal*), to re-occupy the northern part of High Wood. A severely delayed but bold cavalry attack by the 7th Dragoon Guards and 20th Deccan Horse in conjunction with 7th Division (Major General H.E. Watts), allowed the infantry to establish a lodgement in the wood, whilst at the same time the cavalry, subjected to small arms fire as daylight began to fade, were obliged to dismount and dig in on the High Wood to Longueval road and the all-important decisive moment had passed.

The Deccan Horse.

Thanks to the war diary relating to the 2nd Queen's (Royal West Surrey) Regiment, 91 Brigade (Brigadier General Minshull-Ford), 7th Division, we can follow the course of events on that day:

> **Mansel Copse**, *approximately 4 miles south west of High Wood: 8.50am marched to a position East of Mametz Wood & Flat Iron Copse Valley – head of Battalion at S.20.a.2.9 at 11.00am under heavy shell fire.*

The above brief account of an approach march taking place on an active battlefield is a reminder that although the German Army was in some local disarray, it was by no means incapable of hitting back and a salutary lesson that artillery shells destroy and dismember.

> **Flat Iron Valley**: *5.15pm ordered to attack and capture High Wood, 5.35pm Artillery barrage to lift at 6.15pm. 33rd Div to attack at this time West of Cemetery (Bazentin-le-Petit) and seize Switch Trench North West of High Wood.*
> **The Windmill**: *6.45pm **33rd Division absent from left flank**, 7pm advance started – heavy machine gun fire from left flank also*

machine gun and rifle fire from the front by enemy concealed in shell holes between Windmill road and High Wood. 7.15pm right flank to push on following the direction of a track leading to the South East corner of High Wood, several prisoners captured and a lot of the enemy killed, our men shooting them from the standing position whenever they got a target. 7.25pm, after advancing 700 yards, C&D Companies captured 3 of 77mm field guns [the breech blocks had been removed, a standard procedure to render an abandoned gun useless to the enemy.*] The cavalry and an aeroplane assisted in our advance, the former by engaging the enemy on our right flank and the latter by dropping to a height of about 500 feet & firing into the enemy between our front line & High Wood. 8.10pm C+D Companies reached a track running N.W. to S.E. through the centre of High Wood, green signal flares lit to signal this position to a contact aeroplane.*

***91 Brigade Machine Gun Company's** 8 guns sent to High Wood to consolidate the position. HIGH WOOD only partially taken and the enemy made several counter attacks during the night. Reinforcements sent to HIGH WOOD to replace 15 casualties – but for the assistance rendered by the gun teams the wood would probably have been abandoned. Infantry retreated several times from the West of the wood. [The times of events* were mostly omitted in this diary.*]*

2nd Battalion Queen's Royal Regiment (West Surrey) War Diary continued:

8.45pm Final objective gained the North East corner of High Wood where trenches were dug. Several dugouts were cleared by the Company Bombers including one which contained a doctor and several more prisoners.

*11.30pm Enemy made a counter attack from North West corner of the wood, driven back by machine gun, Lewis gun & rifle fire, left flank now in the air [*exposed and unsupported*], 2nd Lieutenant Rutter being killed leading a platoon of B Company during this action.*

Second Lieutenant Frank Lionel Rutter (22) was resident in London; to

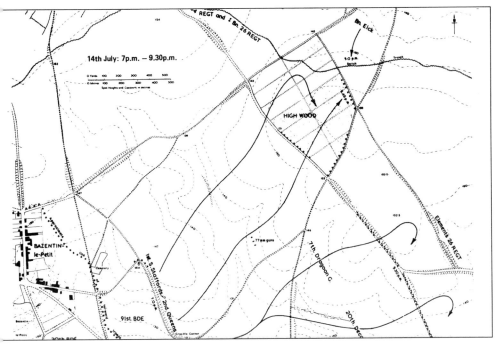

High Wood 7pm – 9.30pm, 14 July 1916)

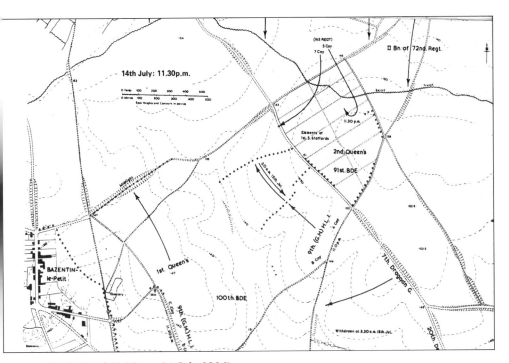

High Wood 11.30pm, 14 July 1916)

date his body has not been identified, therefore his name is recorded on the Thiepval Memorial. A total of twenty-four soldiers of the 2nd Queens are recorded as killed on 14 July, with probably twice that number wounded; perusal of casualty figures for the First World War usually reveals those proportions. Total casualty figures for the troops of the 3rd, 7th, 9th (Scottish) and 21st Divisions for the attack were 9,194. The Germans later commented that:

> The British said in their army reports that High Wood was furnished with all the means of field fortification. In fact the position scarcely amounted to a trench and there was not a metre of wire.

General Sixt von Arnim, who at 9am on 14 July found himself pitched into command of the sector under British attack, later commented that:

> There were no rear positions, no switches, (the Switch Line being only partially complete) no communication trenches and the artillery had suffered severely.

German casualties are difficult to determine, but we can say with some certainty that 16th Bavarian Division lost approximately 2,300 men on 14 July. The Germans also noted that the British had changed their tactics. When they

General Sixt von Arnim

broke into German trenches they proceeded to 'roll up' the positions to left and right, a tactic that they failed to employ on 1 July.

The reader will note in the above war diary entry (6.45pm, The Windmill) the 33rd Division (Major General H.J.S. Landon) was 'absent' from the left flank. By way of explanation for this absence, the north-west corner of Bazentin-le-Petit Wood was not finally secured by the 21st Division (Major General D.G.M. Campbell) until 7pm, by which time 91 Brigade were in action. The war diary of the 33rd Division revealed the reasons for the delay summarised below as follows:

The order to move a division was a serious one for at full strength a 1916 British division consisted of 19,372 men, 5,000 horses, plus motor vehicles. The roads, such as existed, had to be kept clear of conflicting movements and at the same time the vital work of supply and evacuation could not be hindered. The divisional diary goes some way to explaining the complexity of moving masses of men on to a battlefield, which required all the parts of the machine to act as one.

At **7.40am** the division received a telephone call from XV Corps asking if they were ready to move forward from their positions around the villages of Bécordel and Méaulte, the reply was in the affirmative. Another message from Corps arrived at **9.30am** ordering the division to start its forward movement. The details of the plan will be of interest: 'the intention being that, *if the cavalry succeeded in taking High Wood*, [author's italics] 7th Division were to relieve them there'. Upon the expected success of the 7th Division, the 21st Division were to push forward and the 33rd Division would attack between High Wood and the right of the 21st Division. The objective of the 33rd Division was the Switch Line, where it emerged from High Wood, followed by the taking of the fortified village of Martinpuich known to the troops as Martin's Push.

Most importantly for historical accuracy, sometime after **4.30pm** 'as a result of a visit by the Corps Commander (Horne) and a variation of orders originally received from Corps', orders were sent out to stop the forward movement of the 33rd Division, the official written order being issued at **6.25pm**. Meanwhile, 98 Brigade (Brigadier General Carleton) had reached a point south-west of Mametz Wood when orders cancelling the attack were received. By **7.30pm** the brigade was in bivouacs at map reference F.4 and D.

This explains the absence of the 33rd Division, but as to the 7th Division not being informed of the situation, this must be considered as another example of the fog of war and the tortuous routes that signals and messages had to take. Consider that to keep all the corps, division, brigade and battalion commands informed required Fourth Army to inform three corps commanders, four divisional commanders, four brigadier generals and twelve battalion commanders plus Cavalry Corps HQ, 2nd Indian (Cavalry Division) and the Secunderabad Cavalry Brigade. A lost runner or a damaged telephone wire could cause the communication system to fail, leading to messages being late or not

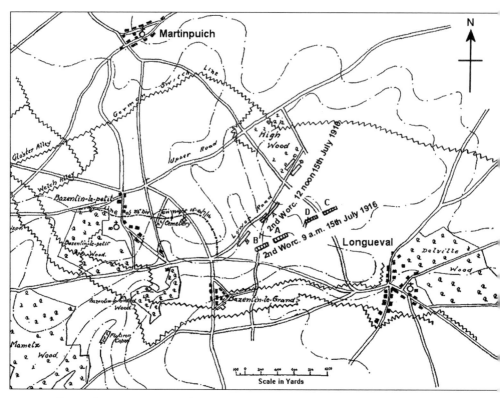

General situation 9am 15th July

arriving at all. This situation, and similar snags, has been described as the 'race to chaos', in which the best laid plans rarely survive first contact with the enemy.

The Switch Line needs further explanation. High Wood straddles the crest of a ridge, which falls away to the north; this part of the wood was invisible to Fourth Army, whose observers were located on the lower ground south of it. Aircraft spotting proved to be the most reliable provider of intelligence regarding the enemy positions in the wood, but even this was difficult to safely interpret due to the close proximity of the opposing forces and the real threat of bombarding friendly troops. When complete, the Switch Line would stretch from approximately 800 yards north of Pozières on the Albert–Bapume road to a point 700 yards south of the village of Flers, a distance (allowing for twists and turns) of approximately 7,000 yards. This trench line provided the Germans with the ability to 'switch' troops in relative safety to threatened areas of the battlefield; it would go on to become a very real thorn in the side of Fourth Army.

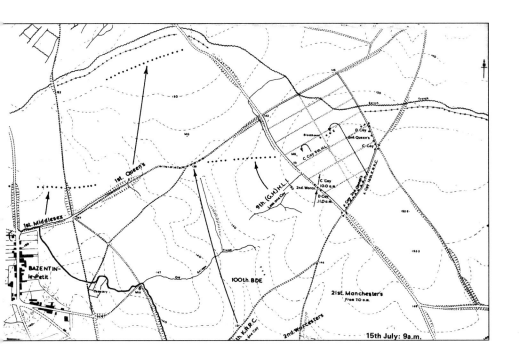

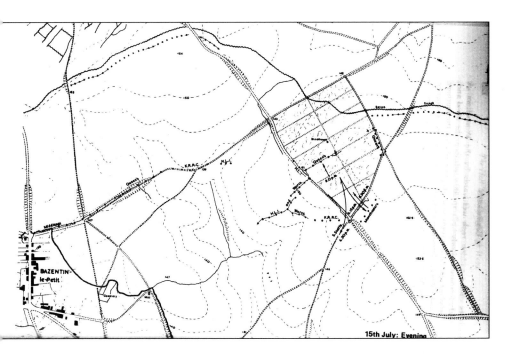

The confusion that enveloped parts of Fourth Army on that day and prevented the taking of High Wood resulted in two months of ferocious fighting before the Germans finally conceded the wood. However, the effects of the fog of war were not confined exclusively to the British. Reports of a British breakthrough were received by the German commander-in-chief, Erich von Falkenhayn, who promptly despatched three divisions to make a counter-attack. The breakthrough proved to be no more than British prisoners being escorted to the rear. The *Official History* notes that alarmist reports were received at German HQs:

> *The British had broken through northwards between Longueval and Pozieres by 9.40pm (8.40pm British time) and had reached the line Flers–High Wood–Martinpuich, and were still advancing.*

Having succeeded in an endeavour that only recently had seemed impossible, to the extent that privately the French had described the planned attack as 'organised by amateurs for amateurs', the close of day found Fourth Army largely victorious, having achieved most, but not all, of its objectives on the Bazentin Ridge. Most importantly for the success or not of future operations, the enemy was once more in possession of the northern apex of High Wood, denying overall observation and control of the battlefield to Fourth Army. An example of the observation still enjoyed by the Germans included the ability to observe movements on the Le Transloy–Beaulencourt road, a distance of 8½ miles. General Balfourier sent a message of congratulations to Fourth Army HQ reading:

> *'They dared, they have managed,' to which Montgomery replied: 'and so the General will not eat his hat.'*

Chapter 2

High Wood:
the Accidental Hell

Saturday 15 July, 72°F, misty, clearing later.
The Germans had made an apparently hasty withdrawal from High
Wood on 14 July and they were already withdrawing their guns to a safer
distance in the likelihood of a British breakthrough. Had the enemy
infantry in the wood got wind of these withdrawals and feared that they
would become the next victims of the constant battering by the British
artillery which had already had a significant impact on the German
defences? It could be that the defenders, or a critical mass of them,
decided that common sense suggested a hasty withdrawal before they
were hit with the concentrated firepower of a significant part of Fourth
Army's artillery, which meant being in the path of searing heat and blast
waves accompanied by whirling shards of red hot steel. Unless copies
of a direct order to the occupants of High Wood to retire ever comes to
light we shall never know.

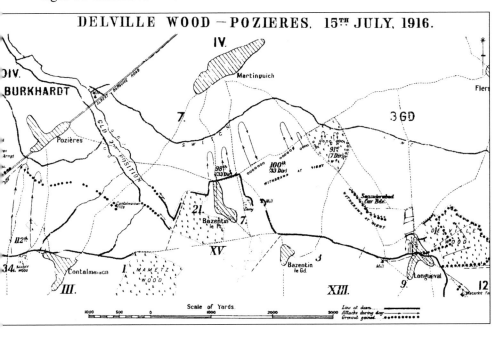

DELVILLE WOOD – POZIERES. 15TH JULY, 1916.

Even so, in the early morning of 15 July the situation of the 7th Division and their cavalry comrades lodged in and close by High Wood could only be described as precarious. Due to the proximity of the Switch Line, (see above map) the Germans had been able to re-occupy the northern apex of the wood. The attack by 33rd Division had failed to materialise the previous day and, with Delville Wood to the south-east remaining in enemy hands, the British troops found themselves under fire from three sides. With the enemy also in occupation of Wood Lane, which today still runs south-east from the eastern corner of High Wood, the British were facing the very real possibility of waiting in a trap that was about to be sprung.

From that day onwards and for two whole months, High Wood came to dominate the thinking of the British High Command in the Somme sector. As quickly became apparent, every forward move attempted by Fourth Army in this sector of the Somme battlefield would be disrupted with heavy loss by enemy fire directed from a wood that occupied most favourable ground for the defence. It straddled a crest on the high point of the ridge on which it sat, thus offering a looming presence with observation over vast areas of the battlefield.

The situation that unfolded for the 33rd and 7th Divisions is described below from the perspective of two attacking brigades, 93 (7th Division) and 98 (33rd Division). Although a brigade headquarters was not situated in the immediate front line area, conditions there were often rudimentary and their war diaries written in difficult conditions. The extract below has minor corrections of grammar and punctuation. The timings are as registered by the headquarters – so that an event that is being described could have happened some considerable time before, given the great difficulties with communications that were a prominent feature of the First World War. Although written in a dispassionate and rather clinical fashion, their diaries give immediacy to events and illustrate the difficulties under which commanders of brigades and divisions operated.

The reader will note that there is no mention of telephone lines being used, only vulnerable runners and visual signalling, the latter requiring the sender and recipient to be in view. If the signallers could see each other then so could the enemy. The smoke and dust clouds thrown up by exploding shells would seriously impede the reliability of visual signalling. A note book, compiled by Lieutenant C. Lander, 10th Royal

Warwickshire Regiment, from his time attending a battalion signals officer's course, provides details of the procedures to be used when setting up visual communications:

Always endeavour to get visual communication between stations, Lucas lamp is best. Advantages of Lucas lamp are its portability (small lateral range) penetrating power of rays, very good at night. For secrecy, select stations so that enemy cannot read your light, or see that rays are not thrown on the ground which would make it possible to read the message from a flank. To prevent this, when using the Lucas lamp at night, use a night shade. Note: to prevent the enemy reading the lamp, shine the light down a piece of tube about three inches wide and about two feet long.

There were always watchers, listeners and ever alert snipers on both sides ready to take advantage of a single careless act in the race for intelligence. Many lives were lost due to lack of attention to communication security and both sides diverted considerable resources in attempts to 'listen in' to the other's wireless and telephone messages.

Communication Problems
Without reliable communications proper command will easily break down. Modern military commentators describe such situations as 'losing the tempo of the battle' which goes some way to explaining the BEF's situation in High Wood, as reliable communications, the prerequisite for success on the battlefield, were not available. In short, if communications fail then so will the best laid plans.

The war correspondent Philip Gibbs witnessed the dire responsibility heaped upon Forward Observation Officers (F.O.O.) by the battlefield conditions in the High Wood sector. Writing after the war in *Now It Can Be Told* Gibbs relates:

Forward Observation Officers crouching behind parapets, as I often saw them, and sometimes stood with them, watched fires burning, red rockets and green gusts of flame, and bursting shells, and were doubtful what to make of it all. Telephone wires trailed across the ground for miles, were cut into short lengths by shrapnel and high explosive. Accidents happened as part of the inevitable blunders of war. It was all a vast tangle and complexity of strife.

Gibbs went on to record a frantic telephone conversation between a F.O.O. and an unknown caller:

'Our men seen leaving High Wood, shelled by our artillery. Are you sure of that?' A further message informed that 'Men digging on the road from High Wood to Longueval are our men not Boches. Oh hell! Get off the line. Get off the line, can't you? Yes, I have that, "Heavily shelled by our guns." Then he spoke into the telephone again; 'Are you there heavies? Well, don't disturb those fellows for half an hour. After that I will give you new orders.'

He rang off and turned to me:

That's the trouble...looks as if we have been pounding our own men like hell. Some damn fool reports "Boches", asks for the Heavies, then some other fellow says: "Not Boches, for God's sake cease fire!" How is one to tell?'

How indeed; enormous responsibility was heaped upon the F.O.O.s despite garbled and often contradictory messages They were charged with executing complicated fire plans and at the same time protecting their infantry, and not from a comfortable office, more likely a hole in the ground open to all the whims of Mother Nature plus, anything the ingenuity of man could throw at them.

Philip Gibbs (1877-1962) was a journalist working in London prior to the First World War. He eventually became one of five official war correspondents accredited to report from the Western Front. There may be some journalistic licence in his work and Gibbs does

Sir Philip Gibbs, war correspondent.

have his detractors but, unlike anyone alive today, he 'was there', and his descriptions of events he witnessed broadly tie in with the accounts of others.

There are many accounts of British and allied soldiers allegedly shot up by their own artillery but it should be borne in mind by the reader that all the armies fighting on the Western Front preferred to site their artillery so as to shoot across their targets (enfilade). By doing so, the gunners could be sure of inflicting more damage on the enemy than shooting head on (defilade). The Germans shooting in enfilade would have been responsible for at least some of the reports of 'friendly fire' – all a part of the deadly dance of death that takes place every day on a battlefield.

From 91 Brigade War Diary, 2nd Queen's (Royal West Surrey) Regiment in High Wood, 15 July 1916

8.00am 91 Brigade: The enemy appears to be well established in the N & NE corner of High Wood. [the Switch Line]

8.27am 98 Brigade: Formed up for attack on Switch Trench.

8.30am 91 Brigade: after a short bombardment by our artillery the K.R.Rs [The King's Royal Rifle Corps of 100 Brigade (Brigadier General Baird)] *attempted to take this part of High Wood (N.N.E.). They were held up by machine gun fire & the attack did not develop.*

9.00am 98 Brigade: Attack launched following a 30 minute bombardment.

10.15am 98 Brigade: Reports received that Switch Trench has been taken [though situation in fact was not at all clear].

10.35am 98 Brigade: Right of line held up by machine gun fire from North End of High Wood.

10.40am 98 Brigade: Brigade on right retiring.

11.15am 98 Brigade: 1/Middlesex report; parts of 100 Brigade have fallen back, Middlesex still thought to be in the Switch Trench 1/4 Suffolk digging in on the crest of the hill, both battalions enfiladed by machine gun fire from the North West end of High Wood and under very heavy fire from enemy field guns.

11.55am 98 Brigade: Suffolks report, enemy snipers, and machine guns operating from a position in front of Switch Trench.

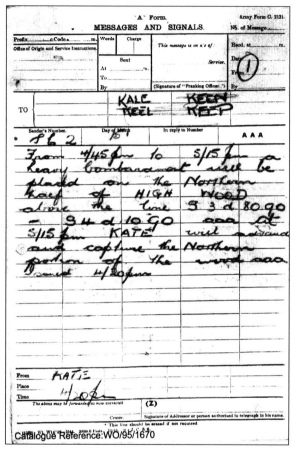

Catalogue Reference:WO/95/1670

12.30pm 98 Brigade: Middlesex report, no men left in Switch Trench, some are in the open between the lines and are being shelled by our guns.

*1.30pm 98 Brigade: 4 /Kings [*King's Royal Rifle Corps of 100 Brigade*] to establish communication with High Wood by means of a chain of runners, visual signals to be set up with High Wood.*

3.30pm 98 Brigade: Reports again received that enemy machine guns firing from the North Corner of High Wood are inflicting very heavy casualties on the Battalions.

3.55pm 98 Brigade: Communication sent to 100 Brigade suggesting a counter attack to be launched against High Wood.

4.20pm 98 Brigade: Report received from 100 Brigade that enemy have retaken all of High Wood.

This report, hand-written on Army Form 2121, has survived informing us of events that afternoon in High Wood. The message can be found in the UK National Archive; WO95/1670, Kate and Kale being infantry units of 91 Brigade: *From KATE to KALE, From 4.45pm to 5.15pm a heavy bombardment will be placed on the Northern end of High Wood above the line S. 3. d. 8. 9. and S. 4. d. 1. 9 and at 5.15pm KATE will advance and capture the Northern portion of the Wood.*

At 4.25pm 7th Division HQ located at Minden Post, near Carnoy, approximately 3¾ miles south-west of High Wood reported: *Divisional Artillery ordered to bombard High Wood, Heavies to fire too. Barrage lifts at 5.15pm, when 91 Infantry Brigade will attack.*

The following entry in the war diary was inserted between the 8.30am entry and that of 6pm: *4.35pm. Our own artillery is shelling North portion of High Wood also shelled D & C Coys, who nevertheless <u>continued</u> to hold this original objective along N.E. corner of High Wood. [Underlines as per original.]*

4.45pm <u>91 Brigade</u>: Our artillery opened an intense bombardment for 30 minutes on the enemy positions in the wood and, on the barrage lifting an attack was made by our troops which was beaten back by machine gun fire. The whole Brigade reserves were now used up and the troops holding the wood suffering severely from enfilading machine gun and artillery fire.

At 6pm an entry describes an attempt to drive the Germans from their lodgement located in the northern end of High Wood. Having advanced a short distance, the attackers lost heavily from machine-gun and artillery fire and withdrew to the east and south sides of the wood. In the meantime, 2nd Queen's Battalion HQ had been established in a shell hole in the south-east corner of High Wood: *'owing to artillery fire the lines were nearly always broken & great difficulty was found in keeping the communications open.'*

At 6.25pm 98 Brigade's diary records that the 2nd Argyll and Sutherland Highlanders *'report hostile sniping from Bazentin-le-Petit Wood.'* This wood was reported clear of the enemy on the evening of 14 July.

The brigade was relieved in the late evening of 15 July. They lost a total of 111 killed on 15 July with a further 475 wounded and 88 missing.

Captain Hutchinson serves his Vickers gun described on p. 26.

At 11pm 91 Brigade records that rations, water and nineteen boxes of small arms ammunition (S.A.A.) were delivered to the companies in High Wood. The diary of 91 Brigade Machine Gun Company, however, mentions delivery of ammunition plus rations and water but *'S.A.A. sent up with great difficulty chiefly owing to the inefficiency of the carriers attached to us.'*

At 11.15pm 91 Brigade records that orders issued to evacuate High Wood by 3.30am on 16 July (in order that it might be bombarded) and withdraw to the HALT (near Minden Post) which was a stopping place on a local light railway. The Brigade Machine Gun Company was also included to comply with the evacuation order.

The German Army was holding on to its lodgement in the northern corner of High Wood with great determination. Only heavy and sustained artillery fire would have any hope of clearing the enemy from the wood, providing two great difficulties to be faced by those conducting the British side of the battle which led to the reluctant decision to evacuate the wood – that of ensuring accurate artillery fire and establishing reliable communications.

The 1st Battalion South Staffordshire Regiment held the apex of the British position in High Wood, under shell fire from three sides and suffering thirst and hunger due to the difficulties of supply. The regimental history is quoted here verbatim:

Eagerly they looked for fresh reinforcements to come up on their flank, but none came – detachments of the brigade dug in, determined to hold the position at all costs – orders received to withdraw at 2.30am on 16 July – 1/South Staffs given the 'honour' of providing the rear guard – the enemy suspected that something was afoot opened a heavy bombardment followed by an attack which the Staffords drove off. High Wood was now clear of British troops allowing the Staffords to withdraw, during which manoeuvre they were confronted by an enemy barrage blocking their way, luckily, for some unknown reason, the enemy had left a gap in his wall of steel allowing the rear guard to escape – they had proudly held on till ordered to fall back.

The war diary of 100 Brigade (33rd Division) covering 15 July is quoted below. Handwritten in pencil and showing signs of composition under stress, the diary conveys a picture as events unfolded that day as well as the diarist's own feelings as far as he was able, knowing that higher ranks would at some time read his work.

S.2.a. 3.2 (Army map reference) 15 July, 1/Queens [Queen's Royal West Surrey Regiment] *and 9/H.L.I.* [Highland Light

Infantry] sent up to occupy the line on the left of 91 Brigade. Both these battalions suffered [illegible] casualties from fire of the enemy in the Northern end of High Wood. High Wood was reported as entirely held by 7th Division. 100 Brigade attacked the Switch Line West of High Wood. Attack by 9/H.L.I. held up by machine gun fire from North West corner of High Wood which was strongly held by Germans and also by fire from Switch Trench North of High Wood which was untouched by our bombardment. 1/Queens held up by uncut wire breast high and both these battalions suffered very heavy casualties....16 / KRRC [King's Royal Rifle Corps] sent up in support of 9/H.L.I. into High Wood and West of High Wood were unable to make further progress and also suffered very heavy casualties from machine gun and shell fire.

The above examples demonstrate the extreme risk to life of erroneous intelligence being unwittingly used in battlefield situations; had things been different, people who today occupy graves in a foreign country could well have survived the war to live out a full life at home. This is not to apportion blame; those involved at the time were continuously operating at stress levels few people today could even comprehend.

To demonstrate how stress in its extreme form could affect people confronted by mass death, hideous wounding, lethal flying metal and noise levels such that the Somme artillery could be heard on quiet nights in South Warwickshire, here are the words of G.S. Hutchinson, a Machine Gun Corps officer writing in 1937. He witnessed the above attack and threw caution to the winds in order to avenge the deaths of his machine-gun comrades and those of the H.L.I. and Queens he had seen being scythed down by fire from High Wood and the Switch Line:

I dragged the gun some yards back to a little cover which enabled me to load the belt through the feed block. To the south of the wood Germans were silhouetted against the skyline. I fired at them and watched them fall, chuckling with joy at the technical efficiency of the machine. A new horror was added to the scene of carnage; a German field battery had been brought into action and was firing at almost point blank range among the wounded. Anger consumed my spirit and not caring for the consequences I rose and turned my machine gun upon the battery, laughing loudly as I saw the loaders fall.

It is a fact that people in battle situations sometimes succumb to the condition known as 'red mist' whereupon, all caution and thoughts of self preservation are disregarded and actions taken that often result in the demise of those so affected. In this instance, Hutchinson was lucky. The role of the machine gunner during the First World War was always a dangerous one. The machine gun was easily spotted by the smoke and flame emitted during firing, plus clouds of steam would form around the gun as the water (and sometimes urine) used to cool the barrel began to boil due to intense use and possible destruction of the steam condenser. It was not for nothing that the Machine Gun Corps had the rather dubious honour to be known by the soubriquet of 'The Suicide Squad'.

Bazentin-le-Petit Windmill, 15 July

Private Frank Richards, 2nd Battalion Royal Welsh Fusiliers, was a regular soldier who survived the war and would go on to write his memoirs (*Old Soldiers Never Die*, Faber & Faber, 1933). On 15 July Frank was on the Somme and engaged in visual signalling between Bazentin-le-Petit windmill and High Wood. For much of that day the Germans were pouring shells into the area and such was the effect of the bombardment that even Frank, an experienced old soldier, began to make strange sightings.

When his friend was fatally hit in the neck by a bullet Frank saw 'the huge black rat we had seen at Hulluch'. Hulluch is approximately 31 miles north of High Wood; a considerable distance for a rat to travel and in this case the 'rat' was out of luck; a shell exploded nearby and killed the poor creature.

Frank and his old regular comrades were tough beyond measure, but constant and extreme danger allied to ear splitting noise and the sights of dismembered soldiers affected them to the extent that irrational thoughts seemed to be reality; imagine then the effect upon newly arrived men from the bases in the UK. Frank was also instrumental in the apprehension of a German spy who had been left behind in the ruins of the windmill to send target information to the German artillery.

To conclude the story of the fighting of 15 July the words of a soldier who was there should be heard. This account was included in *The War the Infantry Knew* edited by Captain J.C. Dunn in which it was stipulated that contributions were recorded no longer than twenty-four hours after the event described:

> *The German guns were splendidly served; the machine guns were sufficient and artfully placed. Hidden by the long grass and covering the Switch Line was new wire and unreported posts which stopped all progress. Smitten in front and enfiladed, two broken brigades ended the day where they began it.*

That the German High Command had been alarmed at the scale and speed of Fourth Army's attack of 14 July cannot be denied, however, the German troops were well trained and resourceful. They had honed their skills during two years of occupation on ground that their government regarded as the German frontier, which the military pledged to defend at all costs. High Wood was the lynch pin of the German 'frontier' defences in that part of the Somme battlefield. The immensity of the task facing Fourth Army involving the capture of the wood was beginning to dawn on the army staffs. For the private soldiers and their immediate superiors, those at the 'point of the lance' who had to face crossing the shell and bullet-swept, coverless approaches to High Wood, their accounts tell of the development of a deep foreboding at the coming prospect.

Sunday 16 July, 78°F, slight rain and overcast
2.20am 91 Brigade, 2/Queens, Coys ordered to evacuate their positions in High Wood by 2.40am, but owing to machine gun fire & the number of rockets fired by the enemy at this time, C & D Coys could only move at a very slow rate & frequently had to lie down while the enemy's machine guns played over them. The Battalion was clear of High Wood by 3.30am all wounded evacuated & battalion marched via S.10. a. Central to Mametz Village and to Mansel Copse.

6.00am 91 Brigade, Battalion bivouacked in valley North of Mansel Copse, the Brigade Machine Gun Company being sent to 'Hidden Wood' [this wood is located ⁵/₈ths of a mile south-east of the village of Mametz].

Conditions on the Battlefield

As the battle had raged for two weeks and the hot summer weather went on, so the physical conditions on the battlefield began to deteriorate bringing in its wake extremes of discomfort in the forms of disease and severe thirst. The 'Blue Bottle' fly (*Calliphora Vomitoria*) soon made its presence felt, specializing as it does in the consumption of dead and decaying flesh. With so many unburied corpses scattered like falling leaves, the bluebottles were offered an ideal food source and a breeding ground, a situation that they exploited to the full. The flies were neutral, they infected both sides equally, carrying with them a whole host of potentially fatal diseases including cholera, intestinal parasitic worms and typhoid. To survive, men resorted to tying handkerchiefs over the mouth and nose in an effort to prevent infection. Sentry duty became an even more onerous task as the flies naturally settle on stationery objects. Even the fact of men having to exist in an area devoid of running water and toilets contributed to the dangers of infection when the products of 'calls of nature' were spread far and wide by exploding shells.

Thirst was a major enemy and exacerbated by the weather and the battle. All water had to be carried up to the front lines, usually in two-gallon petrol containers; as a single gallon of water weighs 10lbs, each container weighed in excess of 20lbs. As some of the trenches used were known to be only 2ft deep, the task of staying alive to deliver the water can easily be imagined, and that is assuming that the carrying party were not killed or wounded on the way. The thousands of shell bursts created huge dust clouds, which together with the inevitable smoke, further increased the men's raging thirsts.

Hunger was itself not unknown even for the British who had ample supplies. There were occasions when ration parties got lost in the maze of trenches or worse, were wiped out by artillery fire. For the Germans, hunger became a repeated concern as the Royal Artillery and the Machine Gun Corps developed techniques that disrupted supply, often for several days on end. Hunger and thirst will sap the morale of even the finest troops, human nature quickly moves from collective endeavour to individual survival. The importance a drink of water and a feed of bread and cheese ('Dog and Maggot' to the British Tommy) to the war aims of national governments cannot be overstated.

Wednesday/Thursday 19/20 July 1916

XV Corps war diary for Wednesday 19 July records: *'Weather much better'*. The preceding days had been overcast and wet which would have greatly impeded artillery observation. The same diary in its entry for 18 July records: *'Postponement of attack due to weather.'* These few terse words illustrate the stage of development reached by the artillery at that time during the Somme fighting, without some form of observation when attacking, the gunners were essentially blindfolded and unable to accurately correct the fall of shot. 'Predicted' artillery fire was over a year in the future, coming into use with great effect at the Battle of Cambrai on 20 November 1917. For clarity the war diary entries begin in bold type, author's notes etc. are expressed in standard type.

Heilly, located approximately 13½ miles as the crow flies, south-west of High Wood:

> **7.0am XV Corps**: *Operation Order No.23 issued, objectives include, The Switch Line and High Wood plus formation of a defensive flank with XIII Corps at Delville Wood.*
>
> **9.0am XV Corps**: *Situation unchanged; patrols out last night (18 July) report Germans holding West edge of High Wood, but no wire out. Two German field guns were brought in.*

The somewhat laconic words used above tell us that a group of men had been out in no man's land during the hours of darkness and were able to get close enough to the 'killing machine' of High Wood to record the lack of German barbed wire along the wood's western edge. Further, what was the real story of the 'two German field guns' and how did the patrol manage to extract these weighty pieces and move them to the British lines without the knowledge of their former owners?

> **9.20am XV Corps**: *The Army Commander [Rawlinson] expressed concern owing to 'the danger to us of the large numbers of our guns concentrated in the Caterpillar Valley.'*

General Sir Henry Rawlinson.

This valley runs west to east from Mametz Wood to Guillemont, at least part of the valley is shown on map, 2408 est as 'Vallée de Bapaume'. Should the Germans have broken through from Longueval, Fourth Army

High Wood from the west side in 2007 – possible remains of a German bunker.

would almost certainly have been faced with the disastrous loss of large numbers of very expensive artillery pieces, which themselves represented the only effectual means of blasting a path through the German defences. Therefore it was believed the attack on High Wood and the Switch Line would also serve to relieve enemy pressure on Longueval and alleviate the danger to the Caterpillar Valley artillery concentration.

> ***9.35am XV Corps***: *Orders to B.G., R.A., [Brigadier General Royal Artillery] to proceed to bombard High Wood and Switch Line to the West of it [High Wood] with a view to a possible attack to-morrow.*

So are the fates of mere mortals decided; a single telephone call would unleash a devastating storm of high explosive, shrapnel, gas and smoke shells; a practical demonstration of the 'Final Argument of Kings'.

> ***7.25am XV Corps***: *ref hour of attack. 3.35am is really for 7th Div. and also for your [5th Div? original unclear] attack on the main trench in the Wood. The barrage lifts off the front edge of the Wood 10 minutes before so as to let you creep in.*

The final arrangements were completed by 9.10pm, 5th, 7th, and 33rd Divisions detailed for the attack with 98 Brigade to 'hold the line'.

Thursday 20 July: 75°F. Clear.

3.35am XV Corps: The attack commenced. The weather this morning is fine, cool, and very misty.

7.20am XV Corps: Reports received at 5.25am that the South half of High Wood was clear of the enemy. 5/Scottish Rifles have gained their objective. Royal Fusiliers report they are holding High Wood dug in on a line N.E. to S.E. Fighting is still going on in the North end where the enemy has machine guns. 24 prisoners have been taken.

5.30am 7th Division, Minden Post, approximately 4.25 miles south-west of High Wood:

20 Infantry Brigade attacking Black Road and Wood Lane began their forward movement as early as 3.05am and gained the Southern corner of High Wood together with Black Road. Line got to within 20 yards of objective [Wood Lane] and met with machine gun fire and enfilade fire from High Wood.

Meanwhile, the 1st Cameronians (Scottish Rifles), 19 Brigade, 33rd Division, had made their way past the ruins of Bazentin-le-Petit windmill where the men were issued with extra ammunition and bombs (grenades). An excellent account of the Cameronians' attack is contained in *A Very Unimportant Officer*, the memoir of Captain A.K.H. Stewart, edited by his grandson Cameron Stewart who kindly gave us permission to quote from the work published in 2008. We take up the story at the point where the Cameronians had almost attained their 3.25am jumping-off point close to the south-west face of High Wood. Exploding shells were cutting gaps in the ranks and there was a danger of the troops losing direction. A halt was called to re-organise the attackers which: *'was done as per the drill book… in splendid style and with the greatest precision and exactitude.'*

The sheer volume of noise created by the battle largely prevented voice communication, which in turn delayed and disrupted the assault; many of those who had stood up ready to attack were mown down before they had begun to move forward. The storm of machine-gun fire enfilading the attackers from the western corner of High Wood and also the Switch Line inside the wood, drove the survivors, including Captain Stewart, into shell holes where they remained for most of the day. Much later in the afternoon, Captain Stewart chanced a run into High Wood which he had no difficulty entering and made contact with the

Cameronians who had successfully driven the Germans out of the wood and repelled a counter-attack. In a somewhat unreal moment, Stewart happened upon the C.O. Colonel Chaplin and one or two of the surviving officers drinking tea and reading letters; he mentions this as a tribute to the ration party who had overcome huge difficulties and dangers to deliver dixies of tea and also letters to the company.

> ***7.20am 7th Division:*** *20 Infantry Brigade report timed at 5.20am the line held is the Westernmost road (Black Road). Easternmost Road (Wood Lane) is strongly held.*

The above report reveals two serious points; firstly it has taken two hours for the information to travel the 4$^1/_4$ miles from the front line to Divisional HQ and secondly, the deadly trap sprung when troops endeavoured to advance from Black Road to Wood Lane. As the contours of the landscape have not changed between Black Road and Wood Lane, today's visitors can easily recreate the conditions of 20 July. It will quickly become obvious to anyone attempting this move in daylight that they become silhouetted against the skyline from observers ensconced in Wood Lane, who in turn would unleash a hailstorm of rifle and machine-gun fire. If the defenders of both sides felt they were in danger of being overrun they would send up 'S.O.S. rockets'. These were pre-arranged flare signals coded by each day that called for artillery support on previously fixed lines.

> ***8.50am 7th Division****: Situation report 6.30am 8/Devonshire Regiment advanced to 100 yards beyond their objective to get a better field of fire, but were shelled out and back to their original objective where they are digging in. 2/Gordon Highlanders are reported to have advanced to their final objective. Situation in HIGH WOOD involved [sic].*

Note that two hours and twenty minutes have now elapsed between the time of the original report and reception at 7th Division HQ. Given the length of time for a single message to travel one way, the difficulties faced by both infantry and their protectors in the artillery show up starkly. In the confused fighting in High Wood, range changes needed instant transmission and reception. With disrupted, or most commonly, severed telephone communications small and instant adjustments to the range were just not possible given that messages received could reflect the tactical situation existing several hours previously. Messages became garbled and the chance of obliterating one's own troops would become a certainty. The diarist of the above 8.50am entry tells us in one short sentence that, *'The situation in High Wood is involved,'* a polite way of saying, complex, complicated, confusing and difficult. And yet these men had to make decisions in order to wrest control of a hugely important location defended by a determined enemy, while at the same time being blindfolded by the 'fog of war'.

> **11.40am XV Corps**: *Had a report that 19 Brigade heard from an officer that enemy were reinforcing HIGH WOOD rather freely from SWITCH LINE. SWITCH LINE was practically undamaged by bombardment. 7th Division asked as to whereabouts of machine guns, whether at 4 b, 5 a, or 6 c, Division to let us know if possible.*

So far, a modicum of success had been achieved by XV Corps, troops had actually gained footholds in High Wood and Black Road but, as ever, the lethal combination of the Switch Line, High Wood and Wood Lane would begin to tell on the attacking British troops. Just who was the 'officer heard from' in the 11.40am entry? By early afternoon, reports were arriving of British withdrawals; in reality the task was just too much to ask. It was on this day at 11am that the son of the Corps Commander Walter Congreve, Major W. (Billy) Congreve, was shot and killed by a sniper. At the time of his death, Billy was serving in 76 Brigade as brigade major. The brigade had attacked just west of Longueval as a part of the prolonged struggle for Delville Wood. The attack had stalled leading to Major Congreve going forward to assess the situation; he was most likely to have been in sight of High Wood when he was killed. Married to Pamela Cynthia Maude only a few weeks previously on 1 June, Billy was posthumously awarded the Victoria Cross for a previous action on the Somme. Both father and son were recipients of the VC.

> **12.10pm XV Corps**: *Report received from 33rd Division that the enemy, after a heavy bombardment, have recaptured nearly all HIGH WOOD. The 33rd Division held on to a line about 200 yards into the Wood.*

> ***1.06pm 7th Division****: 20 Brigade report at 12.45pm Troops in High Wood have been withdrawn from centre of WOOD and are now holding S.W. edge.*

Yet another forlorn and ultimately unsuccessful attack upon Wood Lane had been made by 20 Brigade during which ill-fated adventure, the attacking troops of the 2nd Gordon Highlanders and 8th Devonshires came under fire from Wood Lane, the Switch Line and High Wood, together with riflemen and machine gunners hidden in the still standing corn. Accounts exist telling that the remnants of a platoon of Gordons did in fact survive to reach Wood Lane but were subsequently wiped out, together with small numbers of Devons who had attempted to dig in approximately 75 yards from Wood Lane. It is to the credit of Brigadier General Deverell of 20 Brigade that he did not attempt a second attack as required by his superiors. Deverell pointed out that High Wood and the Switch Line dominated all approaches to Wood Lane and, until both of these objectives had been captured or rendered undefendable, there was no hope at all of attacks such as that witnessed earlier in the day succeeding. Surprisingly perhaps, to those taught that all British generals were heartless, the Commander of XV Corps (Horne) agreed with him; there were no further attacks on Wood Lane that day. Some time after sunset on 20 July, the remnants of 20 Brigade were thankfully relieved by 13 Brigade.

It was inevitable that the Germans would not take attempts to drive them out of High Wood lightly and before long they opened a massive artillery bombardment of the wood. It was only by the greatest good fortune that Captain Stewart and the other survivors, who on being relieved at 2am on 21 July, arrived safely at Mametz Wood to be greeted by their transport men and several jars of rum. Stewart then goes on to rail against the *'blasted blackguards who try to stop the rum rations using the pretence that the rum taught the young soldier to drink, whereas the absence of rum certainly taught the young soldier to swear.'*

The Germans yet again demonstrated their tactical ability by utilising their Switch Line to regain control of the northern sector of High Wood.

Viewed from a desk today, the battles fought by the British for possession of High Wood in 1916 present a picture of immense bravery and purpose but with a constant thread of disrupted communications and unreliable intelligence. As previously mentioned, 'the race for intelligence' can decide the outcome of the battle. As communication feeds intelligence, the one cannot work without the other.

In another example of intelligence of dubious value, the war diary of the 11th (Field Company) Royal Engineers Detachment for 20 July (time unknown) relates that Captain Thomas, based at Heilly had visited XV Corps HQ together with those of 33rd Division and 19 Brigade and, following discussions, had arranged a 'liquid fire' attack on High Wood. The appropriate detachment complete with apparatus and ammunition was stood by at Mametz Wood. The next day, 21 July, the operations at High Wood were cancelled as the wood had now been *captured by 19 Infantry Brigade*, an example of the mixed and often dangerous messages reaching the various headquarters.

The same unit of the Royal Engineers based at Mametz Wood and charged with the construction of five strongpoints in the newly captured areas of High Wood, have left us a handwritten war diary that contains some observations concerning the High Wood fighting of 20/21 July as follows:

High Wood, circa 10.30am (not dated but sequence of events points to 20 July)

> *From reports gathered from those present, the assault went absolutely as expected, the 5th S.R. [Scottish Rifles]and CAMERONIANS carrying their objective. The clearing of the Wood however, was too hurried, evidently not being taken systematically, the clearing parties moving in compact bodies up the open spaces, leaving many snipers and not clearing the dug-outs. There is no doubt that the enemy retired into his dug-outs, mounted his machine guns and shot down & sniped the parties which had passed through. The construction of the German dug-outs in this district renders throwing bombs down them a futile proceeding. It is my opinion that parties of R.E. should accompany the clearing party, moving in rear of them and blowing in the entrances to dug-outs. The infantry reporting any they find and mount guard over the entrances until the charges are laid. Machine gun emplacements, even if found empty, should be similarly dealt with. This should also prove useful as it would prevent demoralised men from seeking shelter in these dug-outs.*

The anonymous diarist of the above displays all the hallmarks of a good engineer; method and logical progress are the first and last laws of the profession. Hence we have the remarks that the men used the 'open spaces' to negotiate the wood, whereas by implication, they should have combed every inch of the wood in a methodical manner. Our engineer was in fact correct as demonstrated by the fact that men lost their lives because the enemy was allowed to re-group and fight back. However, there exist also numerous accounts detailing conditions in High Wood at that time; two years of bramble growth, barbed wire, shattered trees, new and disused trenches and shell 'crumps' all made forward movement from difficult to impossible, hence the temptation to use the rides through the wood which remained largely clear.

Even with the eventual capture of the entire wood, the ground conditions were much the same. Interestingly, the diarist noted that the 'assault went absolutely as expected' yet Captain Stewart and his surviving troops spent the day in shell holes: a good example of a 'few yards and entirely different war'.

Two further entries should be included here as they have the immediacy of the hour told by someone who personally witnessed the events; it's sad that we do not know the diarist's name, whoever he was, he wrote what has become in our opinion, a history that should be read by all.

High Wood, about 11.30am

No one could tell me exactly what had happened; this would be about 11.30am. The officer in command I could not find and the R.E. were holding the trenches with the infantry. The Wood was reported full of snipers, an enemy machine gun was in action somewhere in the centre of the Wood and the N corner seemed to be held by him. Our artillery was firing short on the E [East] face. An order to leave the front trenches in the E face about 12.30pm emanating from an officer and to fall back to the supports was interpreted as a general order to retreat by many men....They were however rallied and sent back to the E face. Here the majority were killed largely by our own shell fire. By the evening this (shell fire) had accounted for every man in the S.W. face of the Wood. On reconnoitring this area, not a single man was found alive and nearly all had shell wounds in the back.

The diarist goes on to describe the arrival in the wood at about 1pm of the 2nd Royal Welch Fusiliers, (RWF):

Advancing with parade precision under the most murderous barrage, many of the R.W.F. were killed shortly afterwards, evidently shot by snipers..

Reading the diarist's description of High Wood, written in pencil and most likely under fire, it is easy to conclude that this meeting point of two highly industrialised armies had become the 'accidental Hell'. There were countless heroes in High Wood, not in the modern sense where hero has become an overused term, any Tommy who made the dangerous journey from Death Valley, past the ruins of Bazentin-le-Petit mill and came within sight of High Wood, glowering at them from across the fire-swept open country to their objective, deserves the title 'hero'; would that we could record them all.

What were the chances of a successful attack upon High Wood? The answer to the question (without hindsight) must be a very limited one. High Wood was one part of a line of field fortifications that stretched from Delville Wood through Longueval to High Wood and Martinpuich, all covered by the Switch Line. A glance at the map will show that troops attacking Wood Lane or High Wood would automatically come under fire from Delville Wood/Longueval and vice versa; German forces in High Wood could pour fire on troops attacking the above. For Fourth Army, the problem in the weeks to come would be how to eject or destroy a determined enemy who regarded his trenches as the German frontier and was determined to defend that frontier at all costs? Colonel Jack Sheldon in his work *The German Army on the Somme* relates the experience of a German officer in the village of Guillemont, 3½ miles south-east of High Wood on 20 July:

380 millimetre [15 inch] shells fired by a British Big Bertha landed every four to six minutes day and night. The ground shook with the terrible impact and detonation of this giant shell, with a hellish crack, an enormous cloud of smoke and dust shot skywards, followed by the clatter and crash of falling masonry. Men were burned or buried alive and every four to six minutes we knew that we might have to turn our backs on life.

Saturday 22 & Sunday 23 July, 68°F, overcast
SECRET
The hour 'ZERO' is 1.30am on night 22/23 July. THIS IS to be

communicated only to those immediately concerned. No reference to it will be made over the wires.

The above is quoted verbatim from the war diary of the 51st (Highland) Division which would play a major role in the forthcoming attack; secrecy being the handmaiden of surprise, the front line, map-waving staff officers and those who freely used the field telephone system of 1914/1915, were citizens of a distant past. However, it is a truism that in the confined spaces of the Somme battlefield, large troop movements and artillery build ups were difficult to conceal. Only the cloak of darkness and the rule of absolute silence could offer any hope of concealing the attacker's intentions from the ever-watchful, all-seeing enemy.

Sunday, 23 July 1916 is a date that has echoed down the years following the Battle of the Somme. It was on this day that the BEF launched the Battle of Pozières Ridge which geological feature was the key to the southern sector of the battlefield; the battle was envisaged as a 'co-ordinated Anglo-French' action. Given the relative success of the 14 July attack, Rawlinson was again using a night action to maximise the element of surprise. Planned for 18 July, cloud cover prevented aerial observation of the enemy positions to be assaulted. Final orders to attack were not issued to the fighting formations until 21 July.

Meanwhile the ever-industrious Germans had not been idle; they had constructed a new trench of approximately 1,000 yards in length that formed a 'dog leg' some 700 yards west of High Wood. The British referred to this new work as 'Intermediate Trench'. Any chance of success against the Switch Line west of High Wood now required the elimination of this new feature. Rawlinson's Fourth Army was now faced with four objectives in a relatively small area: Switch Line, Intermediate Trench, High Wood and Wood Lane. To overcome these problems a series of four differing zero hours were issued to the attacking formations ranging from 10pm on 22 July to 3.40am on 23 July. In so doing the free element of surprise was lost; a single outbreak of firing could and did alert the Germans along miles of their front, as the attackers would soon discover to their fatal cost.

The Pozières Ridge rises steeply from the River Ancre at the hamlet of Saint-Pierre-Divion, passing eastwards through the Schwaben Redoubt, Thiepval, Mouquet Farm, Pozières, Bazentin-le-Petit to Longueval. From Thiepval the rise of the ridge becomes a gentle slope, but a slope devoid of any cover for the BEF as it pushed forward to the summit of the ridge located on the 140-metre contour line. Rawlinson's Fourth Army assigned two corps using five divisions for the attack. For the narrative relating to High Wood we need to concentrate on elements of XIII Corps (Congreve) 1st Division and 19th Western Division and XV Corps (Watts), 5th and 51st Divisions. The objective of this attack was the Switch Line with Wood Lane as a preliminary objective.

At 10pm on 22 July, XV Corps had attacked the Wood Lane defences from a jumping-off point at Black Road, using 5th Division's, 1st Queen's Own (Royal West Kent Regiment) and 14th Royal Warwickshire Regiment (1st Birmingham 'Pals' Battalion). Concerns had been raised regarding a known German strongpoint located at the southern end of Wood Lane and the possibility of a second strongpoint at the eastern corner of High Wood. The possibility proved to be only too correct as machine guns were subsequently located in both strongpoints. They caught the attackers in enfilade as they crested the rise between Black Road and their objective of Wood Lane and became silhouetted and therefore easy targets. Losses were heavy and the survivors were back in their own lines by dawn of 23 July.

A survivor of that ghastly night who observed the entire course of the action of the West Kents and Warwicks was Lieutenant (later Captain) H. Harrop who was commanding a trench mortar battery and published his vivid account in *Told in the Huts: The Y.M.C.A. Gift Book, 1917*, Harrop's words are reproduced below:

Fritz had a battery of Maxims [machine guns after Hiram Maxim the inventor] *on the corner of the Wood and absolutely enfiladed the sunken road just behind and east of which were his trenches. The distance from our trenches to the sunken road was about 350 yards, all corn and long grass and shell holes. The brigade was to advance and take the sunken road at 1.30am on the night of 22nd-23rd and my job was to smash the guns at the East corner of the Wood. After a lot of casualties among the carrying parties, I managed to get four guns and five hundred shells up to (G) a point about two hundred yards from Fritz's guns and out in the open, well away from the Wood which was being shelled to blazes. We were in the open with no cover of any sort with shrapnel coming over at ten a minute at us. We had two men killed and a gun blown to bits, so we lay and wondered what it was like to be blown to rags. By ones and twos we got to know, and then an H.E. [high explosive] exploded twenty of our shells and another gun went West....*

At ten o'clock we started firing. We did pretty well and were told that we had knocked out several Bosche machine guns, but not all. Fritz was not idle, and his stuff was screaming and banging all round us. Our shells were bursting only just in front, and the rifle and machine gun fire was deafening. The air was solid with lead, steel and smoke, and the flame and crashing roars as the big shells screamed over and burst. The ground rocked with the explosions, and the guns were frequently dismounted. Here we could see men in front and behind us showing up in the darkness against the fitful orange flashes of flame, occasionally we would catch sight of one as he flung up his hands and dropped. At 1.30am prompt, West Kents and 14/Warwicks were creeping past us in the darkness. We lengthened our range, and then Hell was let loose (could it get any worse?) in front of us. The shrapnel crashed and roared in the air and the Boches machine guns rattled, and in five minutes the two regiments were wiped out. A few survivors crawled back helping wounded men along to the rear, and the roar died down a bit.

Private Edwin Henry Streatfield (Royal West Kents) was killed in the above attack on Wood Lane; a waterproof cape marked E.H.S was discovered with the remains during a post battle search of High Wood. Private Streatfield is buried in Caterpillar Valley Cemetery, Plot V, Row C, grave 4. A resident of Royal Tunbridge Wells, Edwin was the son of John and Ann.

Some time after 2am Lieutenant Harrop was caught in the blast of an exploding shell:

There was a great crash behind me and I was hit everywhere. My head sang like a telephone and I saw a blaze of green flame in front of my eyes. I was a mass of blood; the Corporal declared 'You isn't got no blood left, sir nor no left ear.' Clarke dragged me away, the shrapnel still roared over us and I cried like a kid with sheer loss of nerve and terror. We stumbled over dead and dying who lay everywhere until we found an ambulance which took me to safety. Five minutes afterwards Clarke was blown to atoms by a 5.9; he was a good sort.

Few people will have heard of Lieutenant Harrop yet his words should live on. This was not a memoir written years after the event, produced with an axe to grind or to make money. This was an ordinary man who witnessed scenes that would drive many to at least temporary insanity, as he himself was when he was evacuated from the battlefield. Could Harrop's words be food for thought for the visitor contemplating the now quiet scenery of the Somme?

We have seen in the above account that High Wood was now well defended concealing a strongpoint capable of dealing with attackers attempting to cross the wide open spaces of no man's land. The same fate befell the troops of 51st Division's 154 Brigade which allocated 1/4th Gordon Highlanders and 1/9th Royal Scots for the twin objectives of completing the capture of the north-east and north-west edges of High Wood, together with 500 yards of the Switch Line, north-west of the wood. The action, which commenced at 1.30am, met with fierce opposition from High Wood and also from the newly constructed German Intermediate Trench west of High Wood.

In an almost inconceivable twist of fate, 51st Division had not been informed of the existence of Intermediate Trench that now blocked the way to the division's objectives and the Germans were thoroughly alert. The war diary of 154 Brigade tells us in stark reality the state of affairs encountered by the attackers:

The Right Attack failed principally owing to inability to make a thorough reconnaissance of the Wood (the troops were newly arrived in the High Wood sector) which is a mass of shell holes and debris. This resulted in loss of direction and of touch with units on flanks. The 2 right Companies came under heavy fire almost immediately from machine guns East of High Wood. The 2 left Companies had similar difficulties, coming under heavy rifle and Machine Gun Fire from direction half right and also from machine guns apparently hidden in the long grass N.W. of the Wood. The combination of shell holes and thick undergrowth and the men's ignorance of the ground made the task of advancing through the Wood at night a most difficult one.

*The Left Attack 2 Companies of 9/Royal Scots advancing to their position of assembly had to pass through the German artillery barrage in the valley between the Windmill and High Wood [*Grande Vallee as shown on map, 2408 Est 'Bray-sur-Somme*]. The ground is rough and pitted with shell holes. From the moment they started, shortly after 1.30am the men were under shell fire. Enemy trenches were encountered at S.3.d.9.7 and protected by uncut wire. The attack did not get past this point. Both Companies suffered severely from Machine Gun fire from the left.*

The survivors reached their own lines around 3am having sustained 450 casualties. The reader will no doubt have noticed that the eastern corner of High Wood is again mentioned as a major source of danger to the attackers. Fortunately for the visitor of today, Major F.W. Bowsher in his *History of the 51st (Highland) Division* has bequeathed a description of the troublesome redoubt:

The Germans held a strong redoubt in the Eastern corner of High Wood. In this corner the contours were such that there was a depression in the ground similar in shape to a saucer. The Germans had fortified this saucer, and garrisoned it with machine-guns, mostly sighted so as to fire to a flank. They could thus, by firing eastwards from this redoubt, rake No Man's Land in direct enfilade. By firing westwards, they could place an enfilade barrage of low trajectory bullets which swept the rides through the Wood. This redoubt was surmounted by wire entanglements; the tops of the pickets being just visible when looked at frontally and from our foremost saps.

If the struggles of Fourth Army were to be crowned with success then this thorn in the side would have to be obliterated. Plans for a more radical solution to the problem would soon be formulated and finally settle on the use of underground mines that would remove the redoubt in milliseconds.

The 19th (Western) Division fared no better, a late relief by 10th Warwicks who were held up in the main street of Bazentin-le-Petit, during the evening of 22 July, upset the timetable, but no fault could be laid upon the Warwicks who had only been briefed for the attack in the late evening of the 22nd. None of the officers were familiar with the local landscape or the dispositions of the enemy and no time was available for reconnaissance. A detailed account of the dreadful night of 22/23 July told in *Lander's War* (Michael Harrison, 2010) tells of dead and wounded set on fire by the red hot splinters of exploding enemy shells, a drunken company commander who was minus his company, the deadly danger of fire from High Wood and the death in bizarre circumstances of the battalion CO, Major Henderson.

Lieutenant Charles Lander and his wife.

When the 10th Warwicks eventually located the new HQ it proved to be a former German dug-out large enough to 'house a hundred men'. Unfortunately, the entrances and exits of the dugout were placed for the convenience of their former occupiers, that is, facing east towards High Wood from where, with the aid of 'star shells' casting their cold, stark light, a machine gun sprayed regular bursts of fire at the openings. The Warwicks were relieved during the evening of the 23 July, their route out took them through Bazentin-le-Petit where so many of their comrades had been killed and wounded twenty-four hours previously.

The 1st Division was set the objective of the Switch Line and deployed on the left of 19th Division. The division's 1 and 2 Brigades were to attack at 12.30am on 23 July. The 2nd King's Royal Rifle Corps left a detailed account of the events that befell them during that summer's night. Time had been made available for reconnaissance and the troops were in a state of readiness to attack at 12.30am. But all along the line the enemy was by now on full alert following the attacks of the previous evening. At 10pm German flares caught the attacking troops in the open, which swiftly drew a storm of fire, catching the attackers in enfilade from their left. By dint of some very hard fighting, elements of the KRRC did succeed in gaining a portion of the Switch Line but were heavily counter-attacked on both flanks by German bombing parties;

this, together with the failure of the battalions to left and right, left the KRRC with no alternative but to withdraw with severe losses. The commanding officer of the 2nd KRRC, Lieutenant Colonel Bircham DSO had been mortally wounded during the attack. Altogether from 30 June to the morning of 23 July, the battalion had lost some 591 officers and other ranks.

High Wood, Wood Lane, the Switch Line and Intermediate Trench were still in the hands of the enemy. Fourth Army had expended enormous amounts of ammunition of all calibres attempting to neutralise or destroy the enemy-held positions. The very latest signalling and spotting techniques had been employed to no avail. Thousands of lives had been lost and families far and wide found themselves bereft, very often never knowing the fate of their loved one who had disappeared into the voracious maw of the ever-hungry Somme.

Sunday, 30 July 1916, 82°F, clear sky.
Fourth Army called a Corps Commanders' conference for 28 July; orders stated that III, XIII and XV Corps were to attack on a line, Switch Line – Intermediate Trench – High Wood – Wood Lane – Longueval, using 19th, 51st and 5th Divisions; zero hour was set for 6.10pm, 30 July. Artillery preparation began on 29 July with the weather allowing good observation but as Mother Nature is neutral, the enemy also had good observation and used it to disrupt Fourth Army's preparations. Lieutenant Lander of 10th Royal Warwickshires noted:

> *The morning of 30th was quiet and we found the body of 2/Lieutenant Rainbow and others of our fellows who had been killed on the night of 23/24 July. We watched with interest as our 9.2 inch shells seemed to be dropping right on the enemy line we were to attack.*

The 10th Royal Warwickshires attacked Intermediate Trench covered by a smoke screen that had been laid on High Wood in an effort to disrupt the enemy machine-gun fire. The attack was initially successful with half of Intermediate Trench captured with the aid of men of the 7th King's Own Loyal North Lancashire Regiment. The attackers had used the tactic of 'leaning on the barrage', a practice that entailed staying as close as 30 yards from the line of exploding shells which, in this

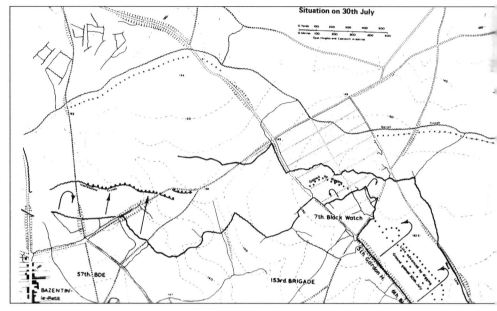

High Wood, general situation on 30 July.

particular case, moved forward at the rate of 100 yards every four minutes; the attacking troops took their objective before the German garrison had time to react.

The Divisional Pioneers, a detachment of 5th South Wales Borderers under Captain Rose, came up to render assistance in the consolidation of the newly won gains which were being heavily shelled. Pioneers were not second-class troops; they were as skilled with a rifle or grenade as with a shovel and rendered invaluable service whenever called upon. Unfortunately, the attack of the 8th Gloucesters and 10th Worcesters on the Warwicks' left had failed due to intense machine-gun fire causing the troops to miss the creeping barrage, leaving the Warwicks with a flank exposed to the enemy.

Due to the linear layout of the Western Front, successful troops could find themselves dangerously isolated if neighbouring formations failed to reach the objective, leaving the more successful attackers to await the inevitable German counter-attack or retire. Meanwhile, enemy star shells illuminated the battlefield and machine-gun fire was streaming down the road from the direction of High Wood and into the Royal Warwicks' positions at the head of the 'Grande Vallée' (map 2408 EST), the previously laid smoke screen having long since disappeared. The much-anticipated German counter-attack eventually took place but was successfully repulsed. Mention should be made of the attack launched by 8th North Staffordshires from the extreme left of the divisional front. A witness claimed that the Staffords were unable to 'lean on the barrage' due to intense machine-gun fire and so lost the all-important momentum which allowed the German garrison free reign to repulse the attack with consequent high loss of life among the Staffords.

The objective for 51st Division was the eastern corner of High Wood deploying the 1/5th Gordon Highlanders and 1/6th Black Watch. The line of the advance followed in part that of the Royal Warwicks' ill-fated attack of 23 July from a jumping-off point at Black Road towards Wood Lane. The attackers were beaten back but managed to establish themselves just under half way from Wood Lane and 200 yards from their jumping-off point. The 1/7th Black Watch were beaten back in an attempt to push through High Wood.

It was the position of High Wood dominating the Somme battlefield, coupled with the flexibility in defence offered by the still incomplete Switch Line, that were the root causes of Fourth Army's difficulties. It would be mid-September before the Switch Line was completely captured.

The losses by the German Army on the Somme are directly linked to Germany's policy of counter-attack which caused severe casualties among her best front line troops and could be described as ill-starred, forlorn ventures which more often than not were beaten off with great loss. The historian John Terrain identified sixty-seven counter-attacks by von Below's Second Army in July 1916 alone, 'and probably many more lost in time's obscurity'. The Germans themselves often used the phrase *Himmelfahrtskommando* translated as a 'Trip to Heaven Mission', or in another variation, 'Report to Heaven Directly' – a mindset not conducive to high morale. As an example of the reality that suffering was far from one-sided in the fighting, German

General Fritz von Below.

sources give the losses of two divisions fighting in the area between High Wood and Delville Wood for the period 15-27 July as 9,498 men.

Chapter 3

Summer at High Wood

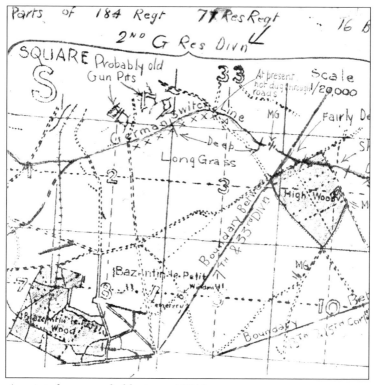

Annotated map, probably August 1916.

On 1 August, 51st (Highland) Division took over the trench system around Black Watch Trench centred on map reference S.10.D.8.8. The division's war diary is quite scathing when reporting the state of the defences as follows: many trenches too shallow to be of any practical use, where a trench could have easily been dug to cross a track none was provided, causing troops trying to cross the track to fall victim to enemy snipers. Argyll Trench was found to be as shallow as 18ins in places and

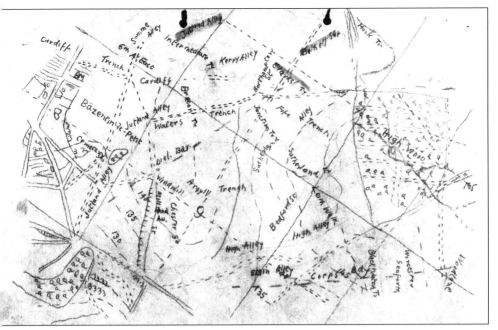

Hand drawn map showing how complex the trench systems became as the weeks went by in the summer of 1916. Black Watch Trench is shown bottom right.

full of dead, rendering the trench useless for offence or defence. The vital matter of intelligence regarding the enemy's dispositions and his intentions were described by the diarist:

> *The information received concerning the enemy was scanty and very indefinite. On our right he was known to hold the Switch Line and a line in advance of this known as Wood Lane which had been dug on this edge of the road, it is not known whether he held a line in advance of this road.*

During daylight hours, British troops in High Wood found that they could move about quite freely without attracting enemy fire. In contrast, at night the Germans were on full alert; the British went on to discover that the Germans were vacating positions in the wood during daylight, only to return after dark.

Early August also witnessed the rescue of two men from no man's land. At 3.30pm on 2 August, Serjeant Russell of 1/6th Gordon Highlanders crawled 250 yards out into no man's land to rescue a wounded soldier who had called attention to himself by fixing his bayonet to his rifle and pushing the bayonet into the ground. The soldier was in full view of the enemy and due to his wounds he was unable to help himself. Serjeant Russell hoisted the man on to his back and ran back to his own front line, being pursued all the way by rifle fire. On the same day, a patrol of 5th Seaforth Highlanders rescued a Gordon Highlander who had lain wounded for three days, all the while praying that help would arrive. Although British troops could move about in daylight quite freely in the open in close proximity to the enemy, being close to enemies in a wood often precluded the use of artillery to disrupt the opposition as the inevitable 'shorts' would be very likely to land on those who had called for the bombardment. At this point (2 August) 152 Brigade recorded that 429 casualties had occurred since their entry into Fourth Army area in July.

The War Diary of XV Corps reveals that a state of confusion existed between the artillery and the infantry who were fighting in the Wood Lane/High Wood area. Where confusion exists on a battlefield, disaster is never far behind:

XV Corps, Heilly, Thursday 3 August. Weather fine and hot. Wind light, north-westerly.
10.20am The Heavy Artillery was asked to stay their fire on German trench East of S.11.d.O.S.8 last night. This request has now been withdrawn.

1.10pm Message received from 17th Division; the Divisional Commander who was at forward Brigade Headquarters wished heavy artillery to cease. On enquiry this appeared due to our men reported to be in Wood Lane. From reports it was thought that either our men were there, or that the wrong trench was being bombarded. Artillery stopped accordingly to allow situation to be cleared up. Later it was found we were not in Wood Lane, and at 4.30pm it was reported our heavies were still shelling our own trench, (the Heavy artillery had not fired here for over three hours.)

Letter received from Brigadier General, Royal Artillery to 3 Squadron, R.F.C., pointing out to them that the Corps Commander wishes them to pay more attention to registering 60 pounder and 4.7 inch batteries on to hostile guns, and that heavy howitzers or heavy guns should not be used against hostile batteries.

> *Lieutenant Colonel Cheap, 7th Battalion Black Watch, visited Corps Headquarters to-day to give a description of the local conditions in HIGH WOOD, and discloses a most unsatisfactory state of affairs. Corps Commander instructs G.O.C. 51st Division, to take drastic measures to put things right.*

The words used in the above quotations may seem overly polite to many modern readers, but it was the language of official documents at that time. In the event, no gunner had to face a court martial, the artillery were acting on information/intelligence received, the gunners never fired on a whim, communications breakdown in all its forms resulted in outdated information being fed to the guns with disastrous consequences for the troops the gunners were trying to protect. The visit of Colonel Cheap to Corps HQ is also of great interest, the Colonel's chain of command being through Brigade – Division. Was he invited to XV Corps HQ or did he take matters into his own hands? In which case his actions point to a man who has tried everything through normal channels and saw no change at all in the conditions his troops were confronting on an hourly basis in High Wood.

> ***XV Corps, Heilly, Saturday 5 August***, *Weather cooler today. Wind north to north-east, 5-10 mph*
> *9.20am 178 Tunnelling Company to get in touch with 51st and 33rd Divisions, and to use pipe forcing jack under the enemy strong point at S.4.d.2.8 as soon as possible. The position for the work is ready, prepared by 152 Brigade in High Wood.*

The above is believed to be the first official mention ordering the use of pipe pushers in High Wood, eight were to be deployed in the wood and one facing Wood Lane. The official title of the pushers was 'The Bartlett Hydraulic Forcing Jack', a device used by civil engineers to install pipes and cables underground without the need to excavate long lines of trenches. In High Wood and Wood Lane the pushers were expected to 'push' lengths of metal pipes at an average depth of 5ft, the pipes were then charged with 2lbs of the explosive known as Ammonal in every 1ft run of the pipe. The intention was, that come the impending attack, a 5ft-deep ready-made trench would appear following the moment of detonation, thereby providing instant cover for the attacking troops.

'Friendly' Fire

The very grave danger of shelling friendly troops, with the severe damage to morale that accrues when troops are killed or wounded in this way, was an ever-present problem.

The accuracy of guns is affected by many variables including barrel wear, air temperature, wind direction, ammunition quality and accurate fuse setting. The design and manufacturing quality of the fuse was paramount to both the safety of the gunners and accurate shooting. If all the above are as they should be there is still the '100% Zone' of the gun to contend with; the shells fired from a single gun will not all strike in the same place, they spread out producing the occasional 'drop-short'. This is a deadly situation at any time but greatly multiplied when engaged in close quarter wood fighting.

A paper produced by GHQ in March 1917 in the S.S. (Stationery Services) series S.S. 139/1 entitled 'Close Shooting in the Field' notes that the 100% zone of an 18-pounder firing at a range of 3,000 yards (roughly Caterpillar Valley to the centre of High Wood) would be 140 yards in length. In the case of an 8-inch howitzer firing at 8,000 yards, the 100% zone would be 280 yards long. Explaining the difficulties of bombarding trenches at right angles (defilade) 'Close Shooting in the Field' tells us the mean point of impact, where 40 per cent of the rounds will impact:

Consequently when shooting frontally at an enemy front line trench at right angles to the line of fire, the best effect can only be obtained if about 40% of the rounds fall on our side of the enemy parapet. In many cases reports of 'short shooting' received from our front trenches would not have been sent in if this fact were realised.... Some rounds will fall short by half of the 100%. This distance has to be taken into account when shooting over the heads of our own troops.... In consideration that the effect of a few heavy shells dropping in a crowded (British) trench, especially just prior to the assault, may prove a morale disaster, it will always be advisable to clear our trenches for the sake of an effective fire.

As the breadth of the 100% zone is far smaller than its length, S.S. 139/1 points out the greater destruction that will ensue if the gun is fired along (enfilade) the enemy's trenches. Each gun issued to the entire British Army carried its own unique set of range tables from which the length and breadth of the 100% zone when the gun was in ex-factory condition; these would be re-calibrated whenever the gun was sent for repair or overhaul. A rather surprising fact regarding the maintenance of British artillery pieces in use on the Somme came to light in the preparation of this work. In the history of 33rd Division's artillery circa 1920, Major J. Macartney-Filgate wrote:

There was a very serious difficulty to be faced at this time; owing to the enormous strain placed upon the guns due to incessant day and night firing, the running out springs began to fail, and great difficulty was found in obtaining new ones. Previously to the war almost all these springs had come from Germany, and, with this source of supply cut off, British manufacturers had found it impossible as yet (late July 1916) to organise their output to meet the ever increasing demands of the War.

The effects of this failure to secure adequate numbers of spares was twofold; after each round was fired, the guns with defective springs had to be pushed up by hand to the firing position; hard tiring work, likely to affect accuracy and which also depleted the number of rounds fired to protect the infantry by 'over one half'. The rate of fire was also reduced by the presence of partially burnt propellant (cordite) left behind in the barrels of the larger calibre guns. The cordite was contained in fabric bags and inserted into the gun's firing chamber behind the shell. After the gun had fired, traces of burnt propellant could be left behind inside the barrel necessitating thorough cleaning to avoid explosion or serious fire, should the next shell and its propellant come into contact with the still hot material from the previous shot. Cordite itself contains picric acid, traces of which remained in the gun barrels and which, if not removed by cleaning at regular intervals, would erode the barrel and seriously reduce the life of the gun.

The 51st (Highland) Division also documented their sufferings at the hands of their own artillery. It was at first thought that the German gunners were firing from Leuze Wood situated to the right rear of the division's positions. Investigation proved that the shells were in fact coming from the direction of Mametz Wood and Bazentin-le-Grand. A party of Northumberland Fusiliers became so alarmed by 'short shooting', as their own artillery were firing over their heads, that they opted to join their Scottish comrades as a safer option than remaining in their own position. On 6 August three sergeants and several other ranks were reported killed by friendly fire; in all 152 Brigade suffered 63 casualties inflicted by friendly fire, 12 per cent of the total for the tour from 2 August – 7 August. Brigadier General H.P. Burn, commanding 152 Brigade felt compelled to put the matter of short shooting in writing to 51st (Highland) Division detailing the incidents as follows:

A total of six reports had been forwarded to division detailing when and where rounds were falling on friendly troops. The 1/6th Seaforths had been *'accurately shelled'* for a period of four hours on 4 August. Over the period of the tour heavy and light howitzer and 18-pounder shells had arrived with frightening regularity. The brigadier ends his letter by offering his opinion the F.O.O. [Forward Observation Officer] did not know the whereabouts of the German lines or the map in use was inaccurate.

On 7 August 152 Brigade left the High Wood area. If the 12 per cent casualty figures given above is correct then the total number sustained during the five-day tour would be 525. Applying the usual ratio of killed to wounded for the First World War gives a figure of 175 killed in action.

An interesting comment appears in the same XV Corps diary for 7 August regarding the Infantry's perception of their Artillery comrades:

XV Corps, Monday, 7 August, 73°F
17th and 33rd Divisions are to send three regimental officers to observe to-days shoot, 5.30pm-6.30pm and again tomorrow morning, 4am to 6am. The infantry between High Wood and right of 33rd Division to be withdrawn to BLACK WATCH TRENCH by 4pm this afternoon and 3.30am tomorrow morning... [and then by hand added] ...This was done so that infantry officers might see for themselves how and where the artillery shoot and help to restore confidence, which infantry lately appears to have lost.

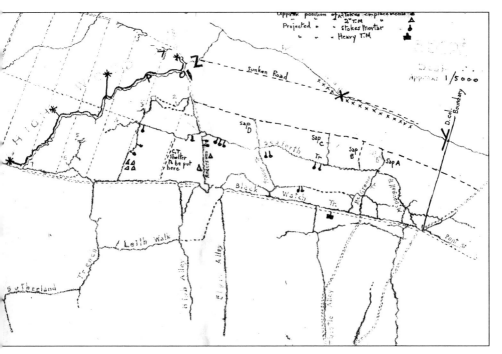

Attack on the Wood Lane defences 11 August (also shows the sap heads in High Wood.

The sad fact is, for all the well meaning of the above diary entry, the close proximity of the opposing lines invited extreme danger from perceived and actual short shooting; a theme which will repeat itself throughout this work.

Most human beings have a limited amount of mental stamina, those that have to live with the constant thunderclaps of exploding shells sent by their enemies to destroy them and having no choice but to observe the results of a 'successful' hit, gradually find themselves mentally drained. For example the words of a German soldier caught up in the maelstrom of British attacks on 13/14 August 1916 ran thus:

> *I stood on the brink of the most terrible days of my life. They were those of the Battle of the Somme. It began with a night attack on August 13/14. The attack lasted till the evening of the 18th when the English wrote on the bodies of our dead in letters of blood; 'it is all over with you'. A handful of half-mad, wretched creatures, worn out in body and mind, were all that was left of a whole battalion. We were that handful.*

> From *Somme Texts: Personal Accounts: Germans on the Somme.*

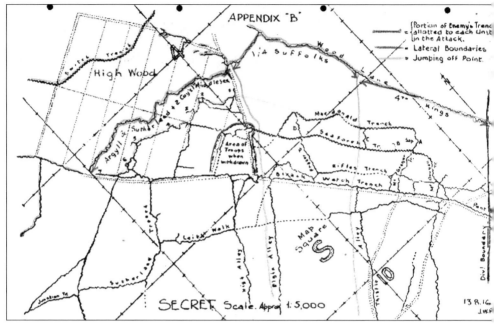

Situation at High Wood on 13 August 1916 – note 'Area of Troops when Withdrawn' presumably relates to an area relatively safe from 'friendly fire'.

Thursday, 17 August; 72°F. Showers with bright intervals.
  Near Bazentin-le-Petit:
  *1/Black Watch attempted to seize Intermediate Trench at 2am
  ...The right and centre platoons failed to reach the objective. The
  left platoon succeeded but was unable to maintain its position. Its
  flank was not seen by 1/Camerons & it was not supported. 1st
  Division order, G 183/17.8.16 received giving detailed
  instructions for a further attack on Intermediate Trench, Zero
  Hour was fixed for 4.15am on 18 /August..... Heavy shelling most
  of the day and at intervals during the night.*

Friday, 18 August. 70°F, cloudy with showers
The seemingly impregnable High Wood still held out against the
repeated British attempts to oust the German garrison. On this day 33rd
Division attacked Wood Lane using 4th King's (Liverpool) Regiment
and 1/4th Battalion of the Suffolk Regiment of 98 Brigade, the Kings

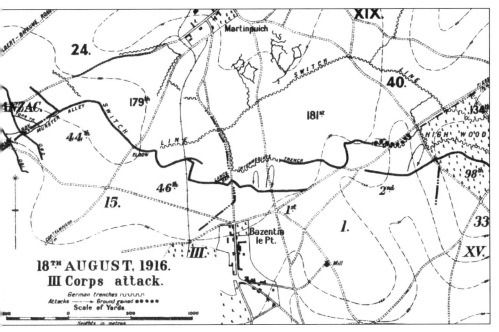

Situation on 18 August – note return arrows where troops were repulsed.

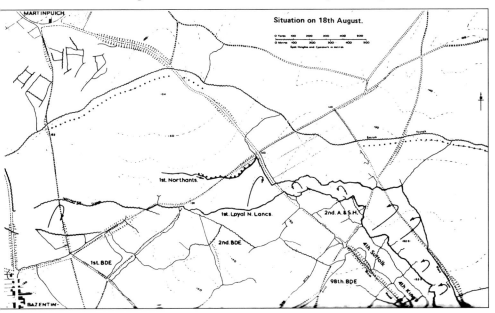

did not reach Wood Lane unlike the Suffolks who reached the objective only to be beaten back by bombers and machine-gun fire in enfilade.

In the same action, the 2nd Argyll and Sutherland Highlanders (98 Brigade) attacked within High Wood itself. Three types of devices were deployed to assist the attackers: two flame throwers, a device known as a Livens Projector, with which it was proposed to hurl thirty-two drums of burning oil into the wood and the previously mentioned pipe pushers for what turned out to be an unsuccessful attempt to aid the attackers. Unfortunately, a downside to these new devices had soon manifested itself – they were very heavy. The flame-throwers alone weighed two tons apiece, plus all the hydraulic jacking equipment needed to push the pipes. To deploy the new weapons effectively, the special emplacements required had to be dug by hand, in the case of the pipe-pushers, one emplacement facing Wood Lane and eight inside High Wood. This was hard, dangerous, and disgusting toil, facing the enemy in a corpse and bluebottle-infested death trap. Although, strangely enough, there are at least two accounts of the Germans ignoring British working parties in High Wood, presumably in the expectation that the same would apply to their work parties. We know that the flame-throwers were broken down into individual 50lbs loads and it seems reasonable to think that the other equipment would have been moved in the same manner.

We can only guess at the fearful turns of phrase expressed by the luckless Tommies allotted the task of 'machinery removal' probably over a distance of 1,000 yards, if we take a point on the British held Contalmaison – Longueval road as the starting point of a journey through narrow and shallow trenches deep in a zone of acute danger.

On the day of battle the new technology failed. The flame-throwers were buried by shell fire, the drums of burning oil failed to make any impression and, although some of the pipe-pushers worked in making new trenches, the *History of the 51st (Highland Division)* relates:

> *The charge was exploded; the resulting explosion blew a fissure in the ground which served as a trench. In this instance the labour of carrying the pipes and ammonal up the line, and the working of the task, proved incommensurate with the results obtained. This was particularly so when it became self-evident that considerable liberties could be taken by working parties without interference from the Boche.*

To the above should be added, that at least one of the pushers blew back down the pipe causing a catastrophe in the British front lines when a mighty blast of flame from the Ammonal, together with accompanying debris, burst forth with a detonation velocity of at least 9,842 mph (some estimates are considerably higher). The initial temperature of the rampaging fireball would be in the region of 2,000°C, enough to vaporise any unfortunate caught in its deadly embrace. All this without warning and in a split second with no time to react, this was no 'damp squib', but yet another ticket to oblivion awaiting the soldier. The war diary of 178 Tunnelling Company, Royal Engineers relates the incident as follows:

> *Zero 2.30pm blew pipes in Sap 2 at that hour, not successful as they failed to blow to surface outside our own lines; blew a crater in our own lines 20ft. Wide and 7ft. Deep.*

The effect on flesh and blood of the explosive force required to produce a crater of the above dimensions is the stuff of the worst nightmare but they were a genuine attempt to reduce the loss of life among the attacking British troops. Not to have tried the devices would have been tantamount to 'a sin of omission', defined as 'every man is bound to do what he can to save his neighbour'. Despite the most determined efforts of the Argylls they were unable to oust the enemy.

On the subject of flame-throwers, the following extract from the war diary of 8 Special Brigade, Royal Engineers dated 15 August 1916 relates:

> *Tountencourt: 15 August, 2pm Detachment of Sgt. Ricketts and 24 sappers with 2 semi portable projectors (flame) proceeded to H.Q. of 25th Division. This party is intended to be used for demonstration purposes to bombing parties & others who may come in direct contact with German Flammenwerfer so that morale of their men may not be affected should they encounter a hostile flame attack.*

The man-portable *Flammenwerfer* (the British often used the German version of the name) issued to the German Army was a two-edged weapon; although fire terrifies all living things it was also very easy to spot from where the destructive flames were emanating and as the range of the flame was quite short, retribution could and did fall upon the operator. There are accounts, not always substantiated, that British troops gave short shrift to anyone luckless enough to be overrun or captured and suspected of operating a flame-thrower.

III Corps deployed 1st Division on the left of 33rd Division, the objective being Intermediate Trench where it exited the north-west corner of High Wood. The 1st Black Watch of 1 Brigade had been in the area for some days and during that time had experienced all the setbacks that could occur when attacking on narrow fronts and under the malevolent gaze of High Wood. Narrow fronts attracted flanking fire, which commodity the Germans were only too keen to supply, and their observers in High Wood were on hand to give accurate directions.

As noted above, 1st Division had Intermediate Trench in its sights, zero hour being set at 4.15am. If this position had fallen, parts of High Wood would have come under fire from two sides thus partly outflanking the menace. The 1st Battalion of the Loyal North Lancashire Regiment made the catastrophic error of walking into the British barrage and being almost wiped out. They secured a lodgement in the north-west corner of High Wood but the 1st Black Watch, ordered forward at 4.15am, were caught in German shell fire. Even so, a small number of Scots pushed out beyond Intermediate Trench but were eventually driven back. A report had also been received that: *'the trench at S.2.d.3.2.1/2 was flattened, one platoon and a Machine Gun Section were buried, and inter-communication cut off.'*

Nothing further was mentioned as to the ultimate fate of the buried troops.

War Diary of 2 Brigade of 1st Division – 'August 18th, Bazentin Trenches:

Brigade in the captured trenches; between 1pm and 2pm it was observed that the enemy were not very alert, to our immediate front and about 400 yards distant from it. There was a commanding ridge, from which the enemy were able to overlook the whole of our trench system – about 2pm a patrol of four men was sent out from our front line trench, and they succeeded in reaching the ridge mentioned above without a shot being fired at them – it was then quite obvious that the enemy did not hold this ridge – two platoons of 1/Northamptonshire were sent up immediately to occupy this ridge and establish themselves on it. Two officer patrols were pushed out and they succeeded in entering the enemy trench known as 'The Switch Line' at two places, both of these patrols were able to advance unopposed and brought back valuable information.

There can be no doubt that at this moment the enemy had gone, and had it been possible at this juncture to have pushed on, the results might have been far reaching. As it was, the troops on our flanks were unable to get on, and consequently no further advance was possible. Between 2am and 4am the enemy counter-attacked us on the ridge; as far as can be ascertained a strong hostile patrol of about fifty men got within 50 yards of our trench but were easily driven off leaving a few dead.

18 August: Attack by Black Watch failed. 1 Infantry Brigade order No. 18 issued: 8/Royal Berkshire Regiment to attack Intermediate Trench, Zero Hour fixed for 2.45pm. Attack by 8/Berkshire failed.

This somewhat terse prose fails to mention the catastrophe that had befallen the 1st Loyal North Lancashire Regiment which had left the jumping-off point a little early and, due to a seemingly catastrophic error, had collided with their protective barrage which proceeded to annihilate them. The 8th Royal Berkshires, who are mentioned above, met a similar fate as they advanced on Intermediate Trench; British shells were (allegedly) dropping short and by so doing, breaking up the supporting flank attack from Lancashire Sap. The frontal attack on Intermediate Trench mounted by the Berkshires was repulsed by accurate and intense machine-gun fire from High Wood and the Switch Line and also by devastating artillery fire.

There is, however, one bright spot to record in this whole sorry affair; the 1st Northamptons gained a lodgement in the trench that ran westward from the north-west corner of High Wood; bombs (hand grenades) were the weapon of choice as the Northamptons advanced from a portion of the trench that had been in British hands from the previous day. Even more remarkably, this small local gain allowed the Northamptons to sally forth and occupy a curiously undefended portion of the by now notorious Switch Line.

The fate that befell the 1st Loyal North Lancashires deserves some attempt at explanation. What we can be certain of is the fact that most visual references had disappeared in the continuous bombardments and barrages. Then add that advancing troops would adopt a crouching gait,

Of Bombs and Bombers

Of all the weapons issued to the British soldier during the First World War, grenades, commonly known as 'bombs' were the most prolific; the bomb in fact became short range artillery. All infantry carried bombs and if not thrown by the rifleman they were passed to the designated bomber. The bomber was a skilled thrower who could often hit a target out to thirty yards. In trench fighting the bomber worked in a team consisting of two bombers, one NCO, two spare men to replace casualties, two bayonet men and two bomb carriers. The carrier's burden consisted of two canvas buckets each containing twenty-four bombs weighing a total of 30lbs for each bucket. Pockets were also used for the storage and transport of the bomb supply, the Australian tunic with its more commodious pockets being reportedly superior in this matter.

The classic shaped grenade was the invention of William Mills, a metallurgist who owned a factory in Birmingham UK; Mills was granted a patent for the grenade in 1915. The Mills bomb, as it became known, proved to be a timely intervention as British troops had been manufacturing their own bombs using the tins of the ubiquitous 'Ticklers' jam as the bomb casing. Home-made munitions are never a good idea and the jam tin bombs were no exception, many exploding, and injuring both maker and thrower.

The Mills Grenade.

The Mills bomb shattered on explosion hurling fragments up to a radius of 30 yards and necessitating the thrower to take cover from the blast. During trench fighting, the bombing parties would lob grenades over into the next bay; wait for the explosion then rush round to mop up any troops still offering resistance. Reports are numerous of forward movement of attacking troops halting when the supply of bombs ran out, leading some in high authority to bemoan the infantryman's lack of desire to use his rifle. However, a rifleman has to squint along the barrel of his rifle to aim and fire the weapon, to

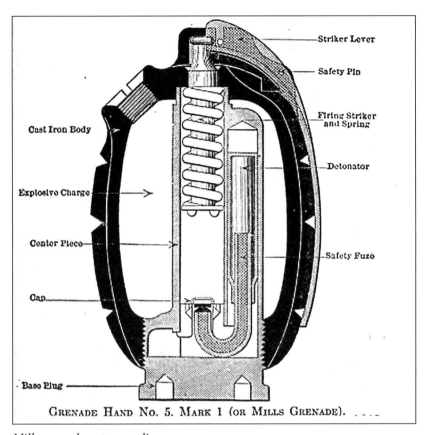

Mills grenade cut-away diagram.

do this he must be able to see his target and his enemy can see him. The grenade spread its destruction over a distance of 60 yards so a bomber even throwing from cover could wreak havoc upon his enemy. The Mills grenade proved to be a portable, relatively safe, highly destructive weapon which conferred on soldiers of relative inexperience, equality with battle hardened veterans of the fighting.

The UK produced 35,000,000 Mills bombs during the First World War and also manufactured a version that could be fired over greater distances from the barrel of a rifle. The original model of the Mills bomb, in size shape and weight, that was used to demonstrate the idea to the War Office still exists and resides in a country house in the East of England.

Grenades are still to be found on the Western Front; they should be left well alone. They could also be found elsewhere; as a 15 year old, the present writer worked for the local gas department in Birmingham and on more than one occasion came across pairs of Mills Bombs secreted behind the gas meter in private dwellings. Looking back, the conclusion has been reached that as the occupants of these dwellings were quite old, they had probably obtained the grenades during the Second World War (not that difficult in that time and place) and being old soldiers from 'the first lot' were determined to take out Jerry 'if he came down our street.' Old Soldiers Never Die......as for this writer? He was told in no uncertain terms to 'leave 'em alone and mind yer own business.'

walking bolt upright being deemed a sure way to get killed. Although, there was a school of thought that believed that by advancing in the upright position and knowing that machine gunners targeted their attackers midway from head to foot, if one's head was where the stomach should be, the bullet intended for the midriff would instead enter the head, result – instant demise. However, torso wounds were in many cases survivable. Not a choice most people would want to make but the only one available at that time and place. Finally, if a soldier noticed his neighbour begin to quicken his pace, his natural survival instinct would insist on him keeping pace and avoiding being a lone target should the whole line speed up. This is not to say that the entire catastrophe was the outcome of an officer whose wristwatch was running slightly fast or a deadly cocktail of all of the above.

Sometime later on the 18th, Brigadier General Reddie came up from 1st Division HQ to consider a new scheme (a proposal to carry out a fresh attack on the night of 18/19th) and report on the situation to G.O.C. 1st Division. As a result of his report, it was decided that no further attacks should take place; warning orders were cancelled. Men who would certainly have died, were given a chance to live as the result of the information gathered by a senior officer whom most of the troops in all probability had never heard of, such is the working of the 'Three Sisters of Fate' who, according to the beliefs of the ancient Greeks, determined the fate of each and every mortal.

In his After Action Report to 33rd Division HQ Brigadier General Carlton of 98 Brigade stated:

I have alluded to the fact that the information I received during the action was scanty and in many cases vague. I do not for one moment intend to throw aspersion upon commanding officers when I make this statement. The difficulty of obtaining good information in such circumstances is at all times great. When it has to be collected from young and inexperienced officers, these are increased ten-fold, and only those who are actually on the spot are in my opinion, competent to judge these difficulties.

The casualty numbers, which I estimate will work out at nearly 1000, are deplorable, particularly as the action was not successful. Among the officers they have been particularly heavy, in 4/Kings alone there were 6 killed, 2 wounded and one missing.

Much as they are to be deplored, they are a proof of the gallantry and the determined effort made by the Brigade under my command.

In his own words, Brigadier General Carlton explicitly describes the dilemma facing senior commanders on the Somme (and all wars before or since) how to make life or death decisions without the benefit of hours spent in multiple, endless meetings, when the top priority was immediate action to fulfil the plan. The anguish caused by the lack of reliable intelligence meant that these men, who could instigate destruction on a vast industrial scale via 'the monstrous anger of the guns' were, even in life or death situations, often powerless to render assistance to their hard pressed troops; a condition known at the time as 'Mental Crucifixion'. Summing up the British efforts of 18 August, there had been setbacks costing many lives. The 'new' technologies had failed to live up to the expected results and in one case actually killed and wounded a number of British troops. On the plus side, the Northamptons had made a small gain which lead to a part of the seemingly impregnable Switch Line falling into British hands.

August 20th, Bazentin Trenches:

Between 7am and 8am the enemy were seen to be massing behind their trench known as the Switch Line, and it was seen that they intended to attack our positions; (strength estimated about 800). The officer commanding our outpost company had been killed during the early hours of the morning and command of the

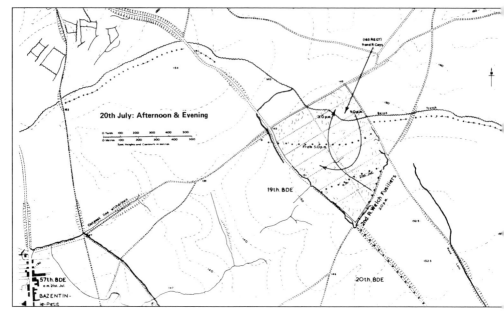

Afternoon and evening of 20 July.

company devolved on a young and inexperienced subaltern officer, this officer seeing the enemy advancing in large numbers (about two battalions) and finding them getting round his flanks ordered the company to retire. The action taken by this officer leaves much to be desired, and he is to be evacuated forthwith from the fighting zone, as both incapable and unfitted to be put in command of men.

As soon as it was known that the ridge had been lost a counter-attack was ordered immediately. Two companies 1/Northants attacked and almost succeeded in regaining the ridge, it being definitely reported at one time that they had done so, it was soon discovered however this was not the case. They succeeded in reaching a point about 80 yards short of the objective and were unable to get any further. The enemy was able to reinforce his attacking troops quickly and easily owing to the configuration of the ground, and he took full advantage of it. By 12 noon the enemy were undoubtedly in considerable strength on the ridge and were occupying shell holes all along it. They were able, moreover, to bring heavy machine gun fire on to the flanks of any of our *assaulting parties from the direction of High Wood and that portion of their Switch Line which was in front of Martinpuich.*

XV Corps, Thursday 24 August. Weather today, fine and warm, good observation.

This day would see the largest operation launched by the British since the 14 July attack. XV Corps was to be in action again deploying 14th and 33rd Divisions. The order of battle for the whole of the attack consisted of:

The French attacking from the River Somme to Maurepas
The British III, XIV and XV Corps.

In theory, by broadening the attack frontage, the dangers from the enemy's enfilade fire would be greatly reduced. Although High Wood was not specifically targeted, success would mean the partial outflanking of the wood which in turn would be the beginning of the end for the hilltop killing machine.

Zero hour was set for 5.45pm but during the long hot afternoon a rather disturbing message arrived at XV Corps from XIV Corps:

Heilly, 2.15pm *XIV Corps telephoned to say that <u>none</u> of their operations will take place to-day. It was ascertained that XIV artillery would be in action.*

We can only imagine the consternation that would have ensued at Congreve's XV Corps HQ. There was now a strong possibility that their troops would be left with a flank 'in the air' and receive the machine-gun fire reserved for XIV Corps as well as their own. Congreve made an urgent telephone call to Fourth Army and spoke to Rawlinson who assured him that the French were all set to go and intended to attack at the agreed zero hour, thereby tying down large numbers of German troops who might well have been deployed against XV Corps.

During the afternoon of 22 August, the 33rd Divisional Artillery, noting signs that another British attack was developing, hatched a scheme to confound the enemy. The historian of the Divisional Artillery, Major J. Macartney-Filgate, writing in 1921 describes the scheme as follows:

Lieutenant Colonel Harris (162 Brigade) had been ordered to position an 18 pounder gun at a range of no more than 2000 yards to enable it to enfilade a new German trench running North East from Wood Lane. Now at 4pm the gun was ordered into action from a shell hole on the Bazentin-le-Petit to Longueval road, due north of Bazentin-le-Grand, at a range of 1,600 yards. Seventy rounds burst immediately over and into the target trench in true enfilade.

Zero hour duly arrived at 5.45pm. The 33rd Divisional Artillery history quoted above states zero was at 6.45pm but for the sake of consistency we are using the times quoted from the diary of XV Corps. Owing to a lack of communication trenches the troops of 100 Brigade, consisting of 2nd Worcesters, 16th King's Royal Rifles and 1st Queen's Own (Royal West Kent Regiment), who would play a major role in the assault, were crowded into the front lines. Casualties were incurred but it was believed at the time that if the troops had assembled in the open then the number of killed and wounded would have been far higher. As if the enemy knew that an assault was coming, the German heavy artillery opened an intermittent fire on 100 Brigade's front at 3.45pm which lasted for two hours when it promptly changed into an intense barrage extending from High Wood to Delville Wood. Did the Germans know of the time planned for zero?

From the observations of British artillery officers, the attack looked to be going well. News came in that the French had swept forward on to their final objectives. The whole of Delville Wood, save a small portion at its eastern corner, had fallen. The above-mentioned gun firing in enfilade *'did tremendous damage, the infantry reporting numbers of dead in New Trench and thereby testifying to the great effects which may be expected of field guns firing in true enfilade.'*

These views will seem callous to many people but, politics and diplomacy had failed, at which point states resort to extreme violence, sweeping people up into situations where, if they do not kill their enemy, their enemy will certainly kill them.

In an effort to reduce casualties 33rd Division had issued an order to 5th Battalion, Special Brigade, Royal Engineers, to blanket High Wood with smoke to coincide with the 24 August attack. As the attackers would be in full view of the enemy watching from his seemingly untouchable strongpoint in the south-east corner of High Wood, engulfing the defenders in thick smoke would deny them observation of the attack developing between Wood Lane and Delville Wood. Smoke or gas shells, unlike the high explosive or shrapnel versions, did not need pin-point accuracy; so long as the shells fell in the general area of the target and the wind was in the right direction success was very likely. The Special Brigade After Action Report relates:

24 August, 7 guns and 300 shells were in position and ready to fire 53 minutes after 'zero' as ordered. A very successful barrage was formed, a thick cloud of smoke completely shutting out HIGH WOOD from the advancing infantry. This cloud must have completely stopped direct or aimed machine gun fire, thereby materially helping the attacking infantry.

The report also stated that *'the two officers in charge had been put out of action',* to what extent we are not told. It should be borne in mind that serving with the Royal Engineers was not a soft option, life could be short, but it has to be said that the pay was far in excess of that of the infantryman.

Meanwhile, the conventional artillery was busy altering the landscape of France and protecting the infantry. The aforementioned Lieutenant Colonel Harris had established himself near Longueval from where he was able to observe the entire course of the battle now in progress and most importantly, he was sending in accurate situation reports that reached the commanding officer of 33rd Division (Major General H.J.S. Landon) much more quickly than all other sources, enabling the commander to make quick and meaningful decisions as events unfolded; a priceless asset indeed.

Once again, problems arose with the technology used by the Army and observed by Lieutenant Colonel Harris reproduced here as per the original:

There was only one disappointing feature in the whole of the attack, and that was the enormous number of 'dud' shells fired by our heavy artillery. Not more than 40 per cent of their shells burst properly, whilst the German heavies obtained at least 95 per cent detonations which caused appalling destruction wherever they occurred. It was a sidelight – but an important

> *one – of the battle, not for many months, did this serious state of*
> *affairs right itself.*

Today's visitor can still come across the evidence of large calibre 'blind' shells, though it takes an expert to identify the original owners of these missiles, they are stark reminders of failure. Taking a dispassionate view of the chain of events leading up to these failures – that is, from the iron ore mine where the guns and shells were born to the moment when the gunner jerked the firing lanyard – was a very costly business. For example, the cost of a single shell for the 14-inch railway gun 'Boche Buster' equalled £3,900 at 2012 values, an enormous amount of money, but statistics reveal that the artilleryman was twenty times as efficient as his infantry colleague at the task of disposing of the enemy. Artillery is a means of transporting locked-up energy of such magnitude, that upon arrival at the target, the energy released will cause mayhem amongst the enemy. What the gunner could not do was occupy the ground he had been instrumental in conquering, which is as true today as it was 100 years ago on the Somme.

The machine gun played a unique role on 24 August when a twelve-hour continuous barrage was kept up on the German lines around High Wood effectively sealing off the enemy and preventing the massing of counter-attack forces. In the After Action Report of 33rd Division, the machine-gun barrage is described as follows:

> *During and prior to the assault, six machine guns of 100 M.G.*
> *Company were employed in sweeping our front with long range fire*
> *as well as parts of the front of 14th Division. They also kept up a*
> *steady fire on the same objective for several hours, after objectives*
> *had been gained to cover their consolidation. The 19 Brigade also*
> *brought machine gun fire to bear on the enemy's front.*

The machine guns deployed were still under the command of Captain Hutchinson who states that a total of ten guns were deployed, firing 999,750 rounds over the course of the action which demanded 100 barrel changes. Coolant had to be obtained from multiple sources including urine tins and two men worked the ammunition belt-filling machine non-stop for twelve hours. The reports gathered from prisoners as to the effectiveness of the barrage revealed that:

The Machine Gun: A Short Explanation
As the reader will no doubt have noted, the machine gun features on an almost daily basis in the story of the fighting for High Wood. Such was the importance of these weapons to both sides that a short explanation is offered.

The Vickers .303 machine gun was the standard 'medium', as opposed to light or heavy, machine gun used by the British Army during the First World War. Capable of firing 600 rounds per minute to an accurate range of 2,800 yards, out to a maximum of 4,500 yards, in skilled hands this was a formidable weapon. The all-up weight of the gun was 51lbs and it required a minimum of three men to move and operate it. The muzzle velocity was rated at 2,440 feet per second: just under half a mile per second. Given this velocity, anyone caught in the open within one mile of High Wood would not hear the 'chatter' of the gun before the initial hail of bullets arrived. Sound travels at a speed of 1,127 feet per second at an air temperature of 68°F or 20°C, considerably less than the muzzle velocity of the Vickers.

The gun was fed by pre-loaded canvas belts each of which held 250 rounds, which at times of pressure or emergency required the crew to change at least two belts per minute. Although steam from the barrel's cooling system was produced by firing, in a perfect world the steam was allowed to condense in a separate container and re-used. If for any reason the crew member responsible for the condenser was out of action or the equipment damaged, then there was a danger of steam clouds being observed by the enemy.

The Germans used a machine gun that was similar to the Vickers, known as the Maxim. Both guns were derivatives of the original gun invented by Hiram Maxim and the performance of both types was much the same. Luckily for both sides during the war, the ammunition used was not interchangeable therefore precluding the use of captured guns. The gun barrels had a life span of around 10,000 rounds; a well-trained crew could change a barrel in two minutes.

The high cost of the Vickers gun prompted the British Government to threaten Vickers with court action due to what was perceived by the government as war profiteering. The case was never pursued as the matter was settled to the government's satisfaction. A direct price comparison with 2015 prices is difficult, but after checking several sources it appears that £4,306 is a reasonable comparison. War is a

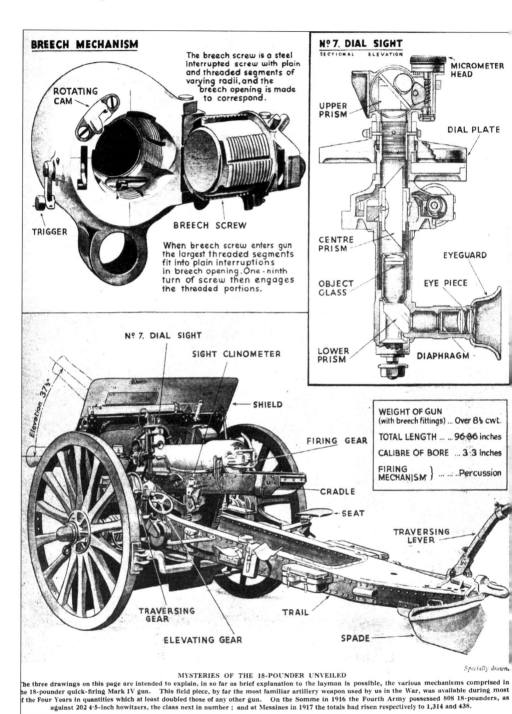

BREECH MECHANISM

The breech screw is a steel interrupted screw with plain and threaded segments of varying radii, and the breech opening is made to correspond.

ROTATING CAM

TRIGGER

BREECH SCREW

When breech screw enters gun the largest threaded segments fit into plain interruptions in breech opening. One-ninth turn of screw then engages the threaded portions.

N° 7. DIAL SIGHT
SECTIONAL ELEVATION

MICROMETER HEAD

UPPER PRISM

DIAL PLATE

CENTRE PRISM

EYEGUARD

OBJECT GLASS

EYE PIECE

LOWER PRISM

DIAPHRAGM

N° 7. DIAL SIGHT

SIGHT CLINOMETER

SHIELD

Elevation 37°

FIRING GEAR

CRADLE

SEAT

TRAVERSING LEVER

TRAVERSING GEAR

TRAIL

ELEVATING GEAR

SPADE

WEIGHT OF GUN (with breech fittings) ... Over 8½ cwt.

TOTAL LENGTH ... ...96·86 inches

CALIBRE OF BORE ...3·3 inches

FIRING MECHANISM } ... ...:Percussion

Specially drawn.

MYSTERIES OF THE 18-POUNDER UNVEILED

The three drawings on this page are intended to explain, in so far as brief explanation to the layman is possible, the various mechanisms comprised in the 18-pounder quick-firing Mark IV gun. This field piece, by far the most familiar artillery weapon used by us in the War, was available during most of the Four Years in quantities which at least doubled those of any other gun. On the Somme in 1916 the Fourth Army possessed 808 18-pounders, as against 202 4·5-inch howitzers, the class next in number ; and at Messines in 1917 the totals had risen respectively to 1,314 and 438.

The 18-pounder, the most widely used gun deployed on the Western Front by the BEF, some 3,144 being in service in 1918.

very expensive means of resolving disputes, leading Sun Tzu to remark that:

Now when the army marches abroad, the treasury will be emptied at home....When the army engages in protracted campaigns the resources of the state will not suffice.'

Costs apart, the machine could fire at forty times the fifteen rounds per minute of the best trained rifleman whose Lee-Enfield would rapidly become unusable due to overheating. The machine gun could also be traversed horizontally and vertically producing a lethal spray of bullets and, as we have seen, the speed of delivery was such that a state of bewilderment and terror would be quickly spread amongst the enemy. The machine gun is just that, a machine, it has no need of rest, food or any other human frailties; as long as it has an operator left alive to feed it parts it will go on working. The unit cost of the gun was high but the protection afforded the infantry by the machine gun in both attack and defence was of far higher value to the successful prosecution of the war. To that end, the Vickers gun was produced in ever-higher numbers up to the conclusion of hostilities.

The effect of the machine gun barrage was annihilating. Counter attacks endeavouring to re-take the ground lost were broken up whilst being concentrated East of Flers Ridge and High Wood.

Ernst Jünger, a German officer who survived and published his memoirs, tells of one particularly annoying British machine gunner (unfortunately, not dated) who regularly caused streams of bullets to descend vertically from out of the sky; *'there was no point in trying to duck behind walls.'*

Heilly, *10.20pm: Situation Report, 33rd Division report they have gained the whole of their objective and are in touch with the left of 14th Division.*

The 14th Division would report on the 25th that they had cleared Delville Wood and were in touch with 33rd Division. At last, for the British, their momentous efforts and sacrifice were showing signs of success. Equipment failures still dogged operations, but communications had held allowing commanders to actually command. As for the Germans, their officers discovered that their own troops had taken to using shell holes instead of the trenches which were receiving a constant battering from the Royal Artillery. This unofficial tactic was double-edged, it was extremely difficult for the British to locate enemy troops so concealed, but in turn the Germans lost immediate command of their troops.

British gains in High Wood were constantly counter-attacked; August saw German attacks in the wood launched on the 12th, 17th, 18th and 19th of the month. The British soldiers who withstood, and most often beat off these attacks, are often portrayed as downtrodden sheep-like creatures driven to their inevitable deaths by a cruel and sadistic officer class. In an organisation as large as the BEF the law of averages would throw up some who would conform to the misconception, but the real figures are almost infinitesimal. British officers were taught to look after the needs of their men first and their own a long way second; had this not been the case, the BEF would not have ultimately triumphed.

Friday 25 August; weather overcast with 8mm of rain.
The 1st Division deployed 3 Infantry Brigade in a renewed attack against Intermediate Trench, west of High Wood from S.2.d.8.5. to S.2.d.0.5. the 1st South Wales Borderers (SWB) being designated for the assault. Their Commanding Officer, Lieutenant Colonel B.W. Collier, wrote a report on the action and it is quoted here at some length. The colonel was present at the scene of the action or very close by and only four days had elapsed upon the completion of his report.

> *At 4.30pm we started a bombing attack down Intermediate Trench from the right flank. We gained about 30 yards and captured 7 prisoners, 8 other Germans showed signs of surrender, so Captain Walshe got up on the parapet, when one of them promptly killed him with a bomb. This took the stuffing out of the attack, which he was directing, and we retired to our barricade, otherwise I think it would have probably have had some success.*

The mention of 'barricades' needs some explanation; the opposing sides often found themselves occupying the same trench whereupon,

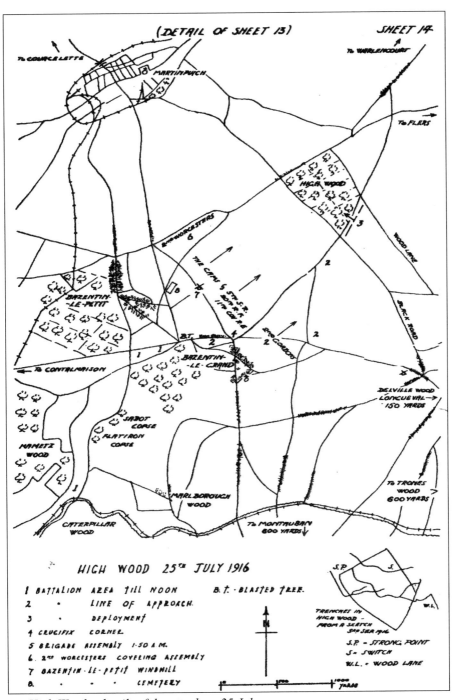

High Wood – details of the attack on 25 July.

barricades would be erected to establish ownership and a watchful eye kept on the enemy.

At 6.30pm we attacked from the same point, with a heavy barrage which lifted by sections (of the trench). In the first two sections no opposition was met with, but when we crossed our own barricade, six Germans bolted from the trench. Those were all accounted for by the Vickers Gun, about 100 yards down the trench a barrier of crossed bayonets, buried in the ground, with their points protruding about 4 inches, and wire strands drawn across the trench was met with. After about 150 yards a Machine Gun was captured. There was a gunner with it who was bayoneted. Afterwards it was found that he was chained to his gun. In the third section 8 Germans were seen lying on top of the parapet shamming dead. They were bombed and ran off before the bombs exploded. They ran towards their strong point and were fired on as they ran.

The above remarks clearly illustrate the menace to both sides of feigning surrender or death. Captain Walshe lost his life because he thought he was dealing with men who were surrendering. In the case of enemy 'dead', the Tommies were by now experienced enough to know that the recently 'deceased' often came back to life and shot them in the back. From the soldiers' point of view, the bombs thrown at the dead would do them no more harm, they were dead anyway or supposed to be. These practices made genuine surrender a far more perilous business than it should have been. It would be the year 1949 before the Geneva Convention was amended to withdraw protection from uniformed troops who engaged in false surrender.

As for the lone machine gunner who met his fate from the point of a bayonet while chained to his gun? There is at least one other instance of this usually fatal practice. The author, Martin Middlebrook, recorded an identical case in *The First Day on the Somme*. Apparently, this was a voluntary practice which included throwing away the key in a do-or-die act of defiance. The body of Captain Walshe was subsequently recovered and buried in Peake Wood Cemetery near the village of Fricourt in grave; A.15. The cemetery is located south-east of Contalmaison on the D147 road. Francis Walshe was born in Suffolk

Captain F.W. Walshe and Peake Wood Cemetery.

in 1879, his medals, including the Military Cross, have been sold realising the sum of £2,600.

Lieutenant Colonel B.W. Collier continued:

It was now growing dark and the men dug a 'T' head for about 30 yards. Three Lewis Guns were brought up, two being dug in at either end of the 'T' head and one kept in reserve. Sometime after midnight, the enemy made a bombing counter-attack along the trench from their strong point located at S.2.d.6.6 ½, close by the Sunken Road, this was driven off. About 3am all the Lewis Guns and most of the rifles had jammed owing to the mud, and it was raining in torrents. Every man was issued with bombs, which, for a time, became the only weapon of defence till fresh guns and Lewis Rifles [sic] were brought up.

Just after dawn, about 100 of the enemy counter-attacked from our right flank but were soon broken up by our fire. It is thought that heavy casualties were inflicted and few were seen to return.

After daylight, an Officer wearing a sniper helmet, with a few men with him, sniped [sic] us with a revolver from a shell hole just out of bombing range. He showed great determination and inflicted several casualties. Eventually he was hit through the head by one of our sergeants, his helmet being lifted off his head. His body was later found. About 3pm a message inviting the Germans to surrender was attached to a rifle grenade but failed to reach the enemy. An N.C.O. and a private then crawled forward for about 25 yards and looked over a mound. They beckoned to Captain Inglis to join them. On the other side of the mound Germans were sleeping in funk holes with no one on the look-out. Two bombs were thrown to wake them up and nine prisoners were taken. The prisoners appeared well fed and had bottles of wine and 'loaf sugar' with them.

Captain Inglis and 2nd Lt. Vanderpump crawled forward another 30 yards and saw a party of 30-40 Germans in a communication trench running north west from the 'Elbow' [a point of the Bazentin-le-Petit – High Wood road]. *They shouted and waved to the enemy to come over; the enemy waved and beckoned our party to do the same. Captain Inglis does not think they had any real intention of surrendering.*

In the meantime, in conjunction with the South Wales Borderers, a company of the Royal Munster Fusiliers had launched an attack which came under a heavy counter bombardment shortly after leaving their trenches; the attack did not succeed:

A great number of German dead estimated at 200-300 were discovered in the aforementioned communication trench and the surrounding shell holes, the Sunken Road in particular being piled with corpses. Operations were much impeded by the heavy rain, but a continuous trench was consolidated.

As previously mentioned, serious thought was being given by the British as by what other means could High Wood be cracked? A suggestion by a 51st (Highland) Division officer in the first week of August, that a mine should be driven under the German strongpoint in the eastern corner of High Wood was taken up with alacrity and within three hours the Royal Engineers had arrived to examine the proposal and duly agreed to begin work on the mine the next morning, 178 Tunnelling Company, Royal Engineers being appointed to excavate and charge the completed mine with the explosive Ammonal. A shaft was sunk to a depth of 35ft from which a tunnel was constructed targeting the strongpoint, the scene of so many British woes. An attack was planned for 3 September, it being imperative that the mine should be ready on time. By 29 August, the mine had reached out 300ft towards the unsuspecting enemy. Next day (30th), the remorseless progress of the mine had reached 320ft and terminated beneath the target; the firing chamber where the explosive was to be packed was also completed. The chamber was then charged with 3,000lbs of Ammonal, detonators inserted and wires led back to the electrically-powered exploder. The final task to complete the mine was the building of a substantial stopping in the gallery in order to direct the explosive force upwards and very importantly, to prevent 'blow back'. For now, the monster could sleep, awaiting the call to arms on 3 September.

To illustrate the importance of preventing 'blow back' a reference to a mine at Hill 60 in the Ypres Salient informs that if a blow back occurred on what was admittedly a larger mine, and if the flame was unimpeded, it would travel for a quarter of a mile in a split second. Any living thing in the path of the flame would be vaporised.

Meanwhile, was the strain beginning to tell? On 28 August, Brigadier General F.M. Carleton DSO (98 Brigade, 33rd Division) had sent five battalion commanders a stern warning which is quoted in full below:

The Major General Commanding 33rd Division (Landon) has expressed dissatisfaction at the progress made at completing the work of joining up the existing gap between the right and left line battalions. While recognising the fact of existing difficulties, he is of opinion [sic] that more work might have been carried out. He has instructed me to say it is of paramount importance that the work should be completed without delay, no matter what the cost or how heavy the casualties, and Officers Commanding

Brigadier General Carleton.

Battalions will be held personally responsible that this is carried out unremittingly by day and night from this time on by parties detailed for the purpose.

No excuse for failure to comply with this order will be accepted.

The very same day, 28 August, Carleton found himself at Amiens ensconced in the Hotel Belfort and writing to his wife to inform her that he had been 'Stellenbosched,' a reference to the South African War and a town where officers were sent who were deemed to be under performing. In his letter Carleton wrote:

I have been sacrificed to the ambitions of an unscrupulous general.....after six weeks of fighting the men had reached the limits of endurance.

Carleton was hospitalised in London and immediately began building a case with the intention of proving that he had been unjustly relieved of his command. To his credit, Carleton was not a stranger to the precarious nature of life during times of battle; two of his officers had been killed as they accompanied him on his tours of the front lines. Very deep emotional agony is the price exacted of many commanders in war and the conditions on the Western Front caused large numbers of senior officers to fall by the wayside. Although not physically present, political pressure was building at home as MPs became increasingly alarmed at the amount of life and treasure being expended for little (in their eyes) discernible results. However, Brigadier General Carleton was sufficiently well thought of by the High Command for Major General W.G. Peyton, Military Secretary to Sir Douglas Haig, to write to Carleton assuring him that he would be re-appointed upon his recovery. Peyton also added a private note:

No report has gone home about you, so as soon as you are passed fit you will be returned to us and re-appointed to a Brigade, but give yourself a sufficiently long rest or you will probably breakdown again.

Carleton was promoted to full Brigadier on 10 October 1916 but he did not serve again on the Western Front. Salonika beckoned, but his health once more deteriorated whereupon he was sent home to take up an appointment at Woolwich. Unfortunately, he found himself suffering from chronic back pain and never again took up an active command. He was heard to remark that the Somme was almost beyond human endurance and had cost him ten years of his life; he died in 1922.

The stage was now set for the End Game in High Wood, lives and treasure would be lost, but High Wood had only twelve days of domination and danger left.

Chapter 4

September: The End Game and the Debut of the Tank

Six weeks had passed since High Wood had stood empty on 14 July. Thousands of soldiers, both British and German, had been killed and many more had suffered wounds to a greater or lesser degree, but all distressing and painful for those concerned. Because of the danger from gangrene and a lack of suitable remedies to halt the infection, the surgeons often had recourse to amputation of the damaged limb. Life was most probably assured although leaving the unfortunate soldier to face a very uncertain future.

Here follows the post war experiences of two British amputees; the first was a professional footballer who had suffered the loss of a leg during the Battle of the Somme. Although he had played for a rich and successful Midlands club, he was informed that 'there is no place for you'; not in any capacity would the club find employment for their former star. The second soldier Private Middleton also lost a leg and upon applying for a position with an insurance company was told 'we do not employ cripples'.

The extended and localised nature of the High Wood fighting would have resulted in large numbers of men facing civilian life at a great disadvantage. Not by any means were all amputations of a surgical nature, the whirling shell splinters and storms of shrapnel bullets could amputate, dismember and riddle in a split second. That is what munitions are for, to drive the enemy away or render him incapable of putting up a defence. In the words of Sun Tzu: 'Weapons are tools of ill omen. War is a grave matter; one is apprehensive lest men embark upon it without due reflection.'

Sunday 3 September; warm with slight rain.
The focus of the corps had now shifted; XV Corps now concentrated on

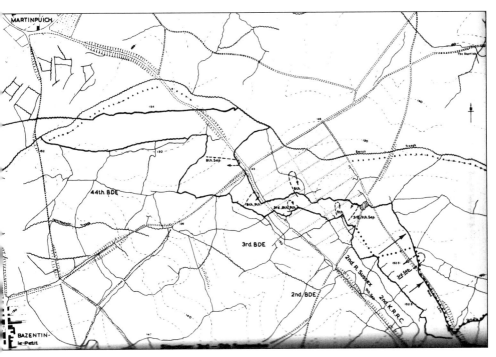

Situation on 3 September showing mixed results.

Longueval and Delville Wood with III Corps targeting High Wood and deploying 1st Division's 1 Brigade for the task. A 'Narrative of Operations' written by the Brigade Major of 1 Brigade describing the subsequent attack has survived and which we have drawn on for the account below:

Zero Hour was fixed for 12.00 noon on 3 September. 1 Infantry Brigade were detailed to attack the German line between S. 10.b.9 ½.8 and the Western edge of High Wood and 1/Cameron Highlanders supported by a half company of 8/Royal Berkshires detailed to attack East of S.10.b. Three companies of 1/Black Watch attacked in High Wood itself with the remaining company and three companies of 10 /Gloster in close support. Six machine guns covered the Northern half of High Wood and four guns sited in BAZENTIN-le-GRAND covered the area east of High Wood. In addition, four Stokes mortars supported the right battalion with six more operating in High Wood itself, each firing 80 rounds from 17 minutes to 2 minutes before zero. Extra fire

> *power was provided by ten 2 inch mortars operating inside High Wood and firing 30 rounds each in the same time frame as the Stokes mentioned above. A sustained bombardment by heavy artillery of the German front lines in High Wood had commenced at 8.00 a.m. on 2 September, continuing for twenty-eight hours till zero hour 12.00 noon on the 3rd. Heavy bursts of shrapnel were mixed in with the high explosive shells; the bombardment itself becoming intense for the final thirty seconds before zero.*

To say that 1st Divison was 'throwing everything at High Wood' should not be taken as an understatement, as together with the aforementioned mortar, machine-gun and artillery fire, flame throwers, pipe pushers, drums of burning oil and the mine were all ready to play their part in rendering High Wood untenable to the enemy.

As the final thirty seconds of the mortar and heavy artillery version of hell on earth began, a Royal Engineer officer some 300 feet away at the end of the mine gallery and out of the direct line of any possible blow back, threw the switch sending an electrical current to the detonator buried amongst the Ammonal in the mine's firing chamber. In a millisecond the ground above the mine heaved and a huge sheet of flame accompanied by a mighty thunderclap burst forth destroying everything human or otherwise in its circle of annihilation which became *'a crater 40 yards in diameter with lips 6 feet high on the average.'*.

'Narrative of Operations':

> *Two Barrett Jacks, although only charged for the last 20 feet, were fired in HIGH WOOD 2 minutes before Zero but blew back inflicting casualties to our Troops of the centre company (Black Watch). A third jack was fired with some success but it did not reach the enemy line. Four Flammenwerfer were discharged seconds before Zero in High Wood and about 15 lighted oil drums were discharged against the enemy. Another set of 15 oil drums also in the centre company were put out of action a few minutes beforehand.*

(Author's note: subsequent enquiries revealed that the oil drums had been destroyed by a British mortar firing short which had also inflicted further casualties on the centre company.)

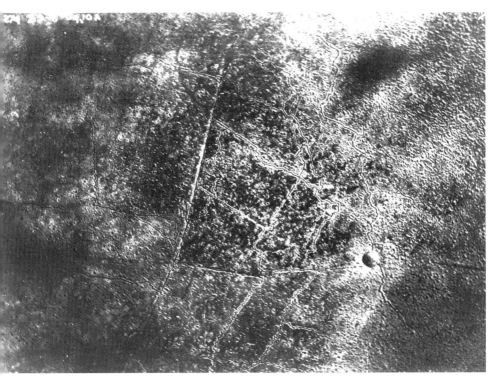

An aerial photograph showing the mine crater formed during the attack on 9 September.

The war diary of 1st Division HQ, as well as complementing the above 'Narrative', allows the reader to follow the course of events as they unfolded on that day in High Wood 100 years ago:

E.9. central 3/9/16

Progress of the attack: The 1 /Camerons advanced to the attack and captured their objective except on the right where they and 8/Royal Berkshire who were to bomb down Wood Lane were held up by machine gun fire. By 1.30pm a Stokes gun was in action against Wood Lane, South of S.10.b.8.9.1/2 with marked effect on the enemy. After very brisk hand to hand fighting in the Sunken Road they advanced well beyond Wood Lane and occupied Shell Holes in a semi-circle just South West of S.4.d.5.7. Unfortunately the platoon carrying tools, etc. wandered too far to the right, the officer in charge being hit. Unfortunately the fire power of the Lewis, Vickers guns and Stokes mortar teams was also lost as they had been detailed to move forward with the now missing/lost platoon, the result being that no strong point was made at

The Lewis Gun: A Short Explanation

As the Lewis gun has begun to appear regularly in the story of High Wood, an explanation covering the history and employment of the gun should aid the reader in understanding the weapon's usefulness.

The 'Lewis', as the gun became known, was the invention of the American, Colonel Isaac Newton Lewis, who patented his design in the year 1911. At 28lbs in weight, the Lewis gun was easily transported and operated by one man, although stalwarts were usually on hand to carry the full drum-type magazines each of which contained forty-seven rounds of standard British Army .303 ammunition. The gun had a muzzle velocity of 2,440 feet per second with an effective, accurate range of 880 yards, extending to 3,500 maximum. The rate of fire varied from 500-600 rounds per minute and the gun was air-cooled.

The Lewis proved to be very successful as a highly mobile fire support weapon for the infantry; so successful that the Germans sought to capture or salvage as many as possible and produced their own handbook to enable their troops to operate and maintain the weapon, classifying it as MG137-e. To have any chance of success, speed was an essential element of infantry attacks and, as the Lewis did not need a gun emplacement, instant covering fire became available.

The majority of the Lewis guns used by the British Army were manufactured by the Birmingham Small Arms Company (B.S.A.) which eventually completed 145,397 weapons at a cost of £165 per gun – £7,104.90p at 2015 values (National Archive Money Convertor) – considerably more than the larger Vickers medium machine gun. The Lewis would eventually outnumber the Vickers gun by 3:1 on the Western Front.

B.S.A. were also extremely successful motor cycle and pedal cycle manufacturers who realised that the weight of tools carried for running repairs was an important issue for their customers. In the light of this need B.S.A. produced small, multi-combination spanners and, knowing of the soldier's dislike of carrying any tools whatsoever, they modified the Lewis to the extent that all maintenance could be carried out using the point of a standard .303 round of ammunition.

S.4.d.5.7. Later a half company of 8/Royal Berkshires came up in support bringing with them a single Lewis gun. In the meantime the Germans began massing for a counter-attack from the north east of High Wood. About 3.30pm the two left companies of the Camerons were forced back into WORCESTER TRENCH. By 4.00pm the two right companies of Camerons were nearly surrounded and about 4.30pm orders were given to withdraw.

Note: Worcester Trench ran roughly south-east from High Wood between Wood Lane and Black Road.

In High Wood the attack did not progress so favourably. The left and centre companies) attempted to assault but were stopped on the parapet by hostile machine gun and rifle fire from the left. The right company advanced rapidly and captured the mine crater. Work on consolidating the crater was at once started covered by a party established out in front. At the same time a bombing party proceeded Westwards down the enemy trench over a distance of about 50 yards. In the meantime a Vickers gun and 3 Lewis guns were got into action in the crater. Unfortunately the Western lip of the crater was very low while the eastern lip was high and all these guns were knocked out by reverse fire from the west of High Wood. The German counter-attack in spite of its losses, succeeded in recapturing the crater and the Black Watch returned to their original trenches.

Fifty-two unwounded prisoners were taken as a result of these operations and about twenty-seven were evacuated as wounded.

The British were meeting with some success as German troops were observed retreating from the area east of High Wood, many of whom were reported as having met their end by rifle and machine-gun fire. Inside High Wood however, matters had unravelled for 1 Brigade. As their troops left their trenches they were met with a storm of rifle and machine-gun fire from Germans who had somehow survived twenty-eight hours of bombardment by high explosive, gas and shrapnel. Literally hundreds of tons of metal which had burst into millions of shell splinters and shrapnel bullets were not enough to convince the majority of the defenders to surrender or retreat.

To German eyes, the sheer dogged determination of the British was becoming a cause for concern. *'They just keep coming'* and *'they are never short of ammunition'* are comments that begin to appear in German accounts of the battle.

And 'keep coming' was exactly what Fourth Army intended, another massive assault being planned for 8/9 September. Not to be deterred, 178 (Tunnelling) Company were already planning to repeat the attack against the German strongpoint in the east of High Wood.

The war diary of 178 Tunnelling Company, Royal Engineers: 4 September 1916 records: *'Investigated the mine; no gas. About 15 feet of the gallery shaken behind the tamping, started work on clearing for another charge.*

With the resumption of work the gallery was made safe and re-timbered as required. Although the skilled miners did the excavation and timber work, they were assisted by, mostly unwilling, infantry working parties. It was a long running cause of dispute that the miners were paid six shillings (6s = 30p) per day as opposed to the one shilling (1s = 5p) per day of the infantryman. Both sides of the dispute are not without merit as all faced grave dangers in their daily tasks.

An added complication regarding miners' pay sprang from the attempt to pay men who had worked in the mines, but not at the coal-faces, at the lower rate of 2s 2d per day (=11p). Great were the protestations of those deemed to be lesser skilled; eventually leading to The Miner's Federation of Great Britain entering the fray. As for the miner, he was expected to work in silence so as not to alert enemy listeners and constantly lived in danger of entombment, and/or asphyxiation by carbon monoxide gas. Many of the miners left their civilian workplace on a Friday and commenced work under the Western Front on Monday. The need for skilled men was so great that no time could be allowed for the men to acclimatise to the sight, sounds, and conditions at the front; these men had to deliver and speed was essential.

A **'Chinese' attack**; the war diary of 1st Division mentions such a manoeuvre taking place on 4 September as follows:

E.9. central 4/9/16, 3.10pm
During the morning our Heavy Artillery shelled the enemy trenches in HIGH WOOD. A 'Chinese' attack was made together

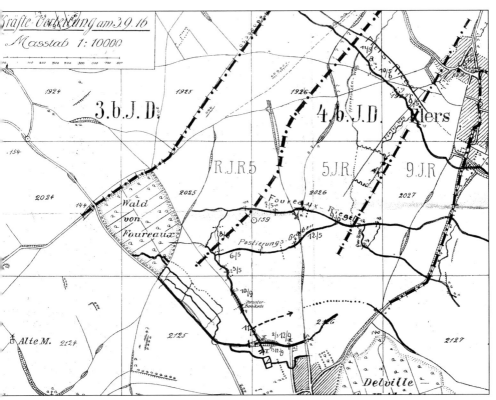

German map of 3 September – note the Switch Line (Foureaux Riegel) is not shown in full.

> *with the discharge of Smoke and Trench Mortar Bombs. Enemy retaliation was not heavy......Two prisoners were taken during the night 3rd/4th while on patrol.*

The 'Chinese' attack has been used throughout the recorded history of warfare. Sun Tzu tells his readers that:

> *If my force is five times that of the enemy I alarm him to the front, surprise him to the rear, and create uproar in the East and strike in the West. The experts in defence conceal themselves as under the nine fold earth; they make it impossible for the enemy to know where to attack. Those skilled in attack move as from above nine fold heavens, they make it impossible for an enemy to know where to prepare. They release the attack like a lightning bolt from the nine-layered heavens.*

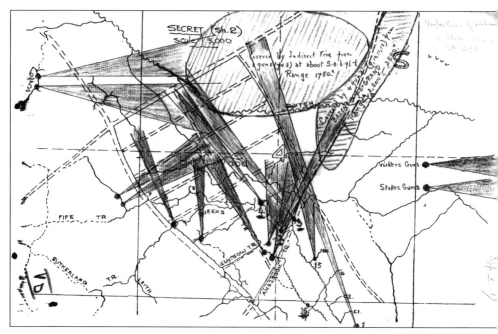

British Vickers and mortar barrage map for 8 September.

Sun Tzu could well be writing about Fourth Army's problems at High Wood and, by his doing so we can conclude that High Wood was not a unique military conundrum. The fundamental problem was that an overwhelming force had yet to be applied by Fourth Army. So why stage a Chinese attack? The prime object of such an attack was to goad the enemy garrison of High Wood to reveal their dispositions, especially so in relation to his machine-gun emplacements or, as we have seen, to ascertain if he was deploying captured Lewis guns. The intelligence so gathered, if applied correctly, could save lives in any subsequent action.

Friday 8 September, warm 70°F, cloudy at first turning brighter.
High Wood still held out against all that an Army that was both highly organised and well supplied could bring against the seemingly impregnable natural fortress. Although German morale was showing the first signs of cracking, at the same time, the defenders were of such a quality that up to now any attempt to oust them would most likely end in a bloodbath.

Zero Hour for 8 September was set for 6pm. III Corps assigned 1st Division for the operation which in turn deployed 3 Brigade for the assault. On the right of the area to be attacked the 2nd Welch Fusiliers were to assault from Sap 4 about S.4.c.6.6 1/2 to Sap 7 at the western edge of High Wood, this would entail a frontal assault with all its attendant dangers. The 1st Gloucestershires would attack from S3.d.6 to 6.9 against the enemy's trenches inside the Western edges of High Wood. The 9th Black Watch of 15th Division were to co-operate and attack the enemy trench at S.3 b.9.2 to S.3.b.8.4. The Welsh were further represented on this day by four extra companies being attached to the Gloucestershire Regiment.

For 178 (Tunnelling) Company this was 'just another day at work'. As their war diary states:

> *Took up 3000 pounds of Ammonal to the mine this morning, requiring a working party of 120 men and 3 officers, report received; drying up of well at X.29.b; we sink further.*

(Note: some words have been inserted as the original document is partly illegible.)

The Engineers had a full programme of work digging wells to accommodate the ever-pressing need to provide drinking water for the troops. If an army marches on its stomach, it cannot march at all without water.

The Royal Artillery began its programme of bombardment and wire cutting on 7 September until 12 noon on the 8th when a slow, continuous bombardment of the enemy trenches commenced lasting until 5.30pm, when an intense bombardment using 2-inch mortars began. Following zero hour, the field guns laid down a protective barrage along the line of the final objective for the attack (S.4.d.9.1 to S.4.a.6.6. to S.3.b.3.8). The account of the action that follows is extracted from a report headed 'Secret' written by the Brigade Major of 3 Infantry Brigade, dated 19 September 1916:

> *Assault: The attacking infantry left their trenches at zero. On the right, the right company of the 2/Welch gained their objective without much difficulty. The left company however, were unable to make progress owing to the machine gun fire from the North of High Wood, and fire from the trench immediately in front of them.*
>
> *The Gloucesters advanced to the edge of High Wood and killed most of the Germans found in the trenches there. They then pushed*

*onwards to the trench [*running?*] from S.4.c.1/2.91/2 to S.3.b.9.2 this they found to be obliterated. The Germans in this neighbourhood appear to have been in small parties in shell holes surrounded by wire and these had to be dealt with one by one. Casualties were heavy, but a few including the Commanding Officer managed to push on to the final objective at S.4.a.2.3 which they occupied after a brisk hand to hand fight.*

The above words, gathered within days of the action, are invaluable to history although by their nature they did not convey the grim reality of High Wood. There was no real need to do so as these reports were only for the eyes of professional soldiers who well knew the sights and sounds experienced by the attackers. Both sides had endured all that industrialised killing could produce, but the final outcome was decided by 'a brisk hand to hand fight', which actually means the protagonists were face to face and eye to eye, where kill or be killed was the first and last rule of survival. Grenades, bayonets, rifles, pistols, knives, knuckle-dusters all featured in 'hand to hand' fighting.

On occasion, a small number of individuals were known to have armed themselves with shotguns for use in assaulting trenches. On 1 July 1916, an officer of the Royal Warwicks is on record as carrying a Winchester Repeating Shotgun with which 'he did good execution'. Shotguns were supposedly proscribed under international law and we have found no reference to their usage beyond the first days of the Somme fighting and then only on extremely rare occasions. These were not normal times and if offered the opportunity to use the ultimate close quarter, trench fighting weapon...would we, in the same position not choose to vastly increase our chances of survival?

Saturday 9 September, 75°F; slight rain

III Corps tasked 1st Division with attempting the clearance of High Wood with the assistance of the second blowing of the mine. The time of Zero hour seems to have been about 4.45pm with the mine exploded 30 seconds before Zero. The 1st Northamtonshires succeeded in storming the new crater but were ejected by a fierce enemy bombing attack. The 2nd Royal Munster Fusiliers and 10th Battalion of the Gloucestershire Regiment could make no headway.

History has bequeathed to us the story of the fate of one Welsh soldier

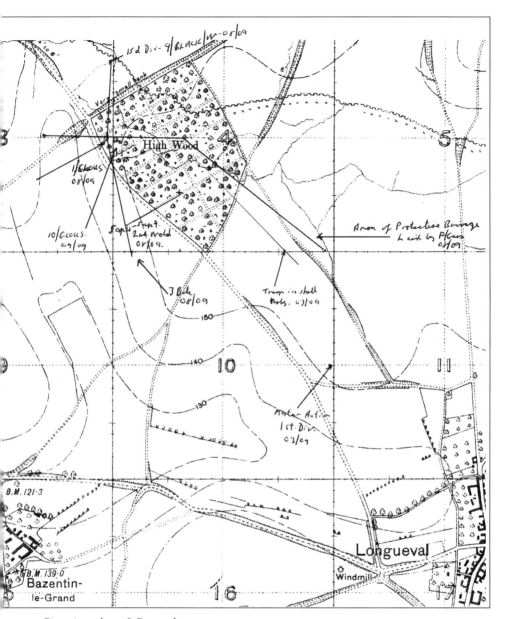

Situation about 9 September.

who fought in High Wood on 8 September. Private Archibald Trevellyn Williams of the 2nd Battalion of the Welsh Regiment was declared missing. His remains were discovered in High Wood in December 1928, his identity being established by the discovery of his name marked on the inside of his boots. Archibald is buried in Serre Road Cemetery No.2; plot XVIII Row F. Grave 13.

Grave of Private A.T. Williams, Serre Road No.2 Cemetery.

Press cutting reporting the discovery of the remains of Private WIlliams.

SOLDIER'S BODY FOUND AFTER TWELVE YEARS.

Information has been received from the War Office by Mrs. Williams, Longford Crescent, Swansea, that the body of her son, Private Archie Williams, had been found and removed from an isolated grave in the vicinity of High Wood and re-buried at Beaumont, France.

Private Williams was killed in action in September, 1916, and the name on the boots established his identity.

Serre Road No.2 Cemetery.

Sunrise at Serre Road No.2 Cemetery. (Photo by Terry Carter)

What do we know of the fighting condition of the German Army on the Somme at this time? By the end of August the sheer amount of *materiel* available to the Allies became an issue to German soldiers. Such was the amount and accuracy of Allied artillery fire that troop movements and re-supply of the forward troops was severely disrupted to the extent that troops going into the line had to carry their own water, enough to last for a five-day tour, during which the odds of survival were beginning to shorten. Few divisions came out of the line with less than 4,500 casualties. The rate that artillery pieces were becoming unserviceable and with defective shells that were bursting in the barrel had risen to alarming levels. Russia was far from defeated on the Eastern Front and by the end of August the German High Command was forced to transfer ten divisions to the East – an example of the enormous contribution to victory made by Tsarist Russia. But even taking into account the dire state of affairs outlined above, the German Army on the Somme was far from beaten. A complete rupture of their front would take a further two years of bitter fighting.

Friday 15 September, 59°F
The Debut of Mechanised Warfare
For three reasons, this is a most important day in the history of the First World War. Firstly, on this day the whole of the Allied powers would strike simultaneous blows against the Austro-German Alliance. Russia would attack from the East. France, Belgium, Great Britain and Italy would strike from the West, forcing the Alliance to fight on two fronts,

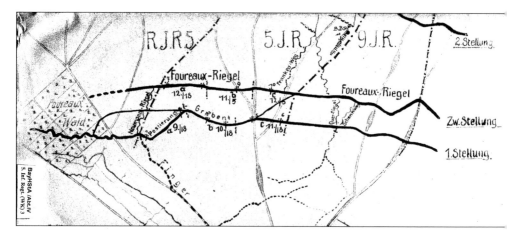

German map showing main
defences in High Wood area
September 1916.

Casualty report of
German division
on 15 September.

*Artist's Impression of MK 1 Tank – the crew have pulled up to obtain directions
and consult the map to find High Wood, a documented incident. (© Robin
Wheeldon 2016)*

which action they could not sustain. Secondly, the day would see the debut of the tank.

From small beginnings in a room over the White Hart Hotel in the city of Lincoln, a cross-country, armoured fighting machine had come from drawing board to battlefield in eighteen months. Though far from perfect, the Mark 1 tank and her successors would change the way in which major battles would be fought well into the twenty-first century. The fledgling tanks and the infantry they were to protect faced greatly enhanced German works within High Wood; iron and concrete had been used coupled with enormous amounts of lethal barbed wire. The numbers of German machine guns active in High Wood were such as to drown out the noise of the exploding shells with which the Germans were 'searching' the British held area of the wood.

Thirdly, this would be the day when High Wood was finally wrested from the invader.

British tanks of the First World War are often compared unfavourably with their counterparts of the Second World War. Caution should be exercised here at least when considering the tank's offensive armament; the 'male' version carried two 6-pounder guns and four or five machine guns, the 'female' five or six machine guns. Although the traverse of the 6-pounders was limited, the male tank could deliver six times the weight of shot of many of its successors in the Second World War which carried one 2-pounder gun with 360 degree traverse plus one machine gun. It is also worthy of note, that the original design brief for the tank was that it should be able to traverse terrain similar to that of the Loos battlefield, which by comparison to the Somme was virtually undamaged. Accounts of British tanks fighting in France in 1940 relate chronic shortages of ammunition, no maps at all and operating without a definite objective.

There are parallels today in 2015 between the first tanks and 'Trojan', an armoured vehicle in use by the British Army. Trojan has a thirst with which her ancestors on the Somme would sympathise, she needs four gallons of fuel to travel one mile. As did her counterparts in 1917/18, she carries a fascine to enable her to cross deep ditches and trenches and remarkably, a version of the 'Pipe Pusher' we encountered in High Wood; Trojan can project a large flexible pipe containing explosives that will disrupt roadside bombs and other hazards. The contention here is to argue that although the tanks of September 1916 were not universally effective, they were deployed in circumstances where success was improbable. The tank's limitations and capabilities were not fully disseminated until November 1917 and the Battle of Cambrai.

The story of the tanks that entered High Wood will be told in tandem with that of the 47th (London) Division which finally stormed the wood. The 47th Division's ultimately successful attack against High Wood is a tale of triumph over almost unimaginable odds; the amount and variety of killing methods that the Londoners and their flanking divisions eventually overcame, makes heroes of them all. Some time before 15 September, the Londoners had been spotted by the enemy who noted:

From 7 September the British holdings in that wood were taken over by the 47th Division of London Territorials, these look very clean and smart and march well.

The Mk I tank, with its soon-to-be-superfluous trailing wheels, cut a strange sight to friend and foe alike. Here was a self propelled, fire-spitting beast that could both attack or defend itself with alarming force by the use of a mixture of 6-pounder guns and machine guns. Much has been written and published regarding the tank's triumphs and failures on that day, therefore only the stories of the tanks that entered High Wood or attacked the Switch Line and nearby locations will be covered.

Forty-nine tanks had left the railhead known as the 'Loop' (6 miles south-west of High Wood, as the crow flies). Breakdowns and ditching left only thirty-two deemed capable of taking part in the forthcoming battle. Unfortunately, knowledge as to the tank's capabilities and shortcomings had not percolated the highest levels of command. The debut of the tanks was marred by confusion, with the senior tank officers (at this time the tanks operated under the title 'Heavy Section Machine Gun Corps') finding themselves ignored and instructions being passed direct to the tank crews by the divisions in whose area they found themselves. Major Allen Holford-Walker, formerly of the Argyll and Sutherland Highlanders, had become commanding officer of the recently formed C (Tank) Company. Many years later, on 22 April 1935, he wrote of his experiences in correspondence with Brigadier General Sir James E. Edmonds, the British Official Historian:

It may seem curious, looking back on the preparations before a battle and the use of a completely new arm that the officer

*commanding the tanks on the front held by XIV Corps was never
once consulted as to the action, movement, distribution, or use
of his tanks. But it is so, I was sent for to Querrieu, the
Headquarters of Fourth Army, to see General Rawlinson. The
only words that passed between us were very short questions
from him as to (1) whether my men were trained, to which I
answered that they were not fit to fight immediately because I
had not one officer or man who had seen a shelled area, (2) the
pace at which my tanks were able to move and (3) the distance
that they could accomplish on average ground and return for
replenishment. Interview Two was with General Gathorne-
Hardy (XIV Corps Chief of Staff) who asked me no questions
whatever but gave me a map showing the pre-conceived tank
routes which had been arbitrarily fixed with no reconnaissance
by any officer who knew anything about a tank at all.. . The net
result of the indefiniteness of higher formations to the
commander of the units was literally disastrous because, while I
was actually in command of the unit, orders were being issued
direct by divisions to the sections but I knew nothing about it
whatsoever.*

The above remarks are quoted from the papers of Holford-Walker.
Although due care should be taken with a narrative written almost
nineteen years after the event, numerous accounts exist which verify
Holford-Walker's words: the chronic shortage of maps which resulted
in some tanks setting out without a map at all, the constantly changing
orders and the crews' complete lack of battlefield experience. Such were
the shortages of even basic tools with which to carry out maintenance
that Allen Holford-Walker arranged for his wife to purchase fifteen sets
of spanners to be sent to C Company in France.

The battle was preceded by a three-day bombardment using 1,600
guns on a front of five miles. No less than eleven infantry divisions were
in place to follow the tanks into action as the complex battle orders were
converted into reality. High Wood itself was to receive a four-hour
bombardment by heavy artillery on 13/14 September. At 6.20am an
intense fire would open on a line 150 yards in front of the British
positions. Reading the orders sent to 140 Brigade (47th Division) gives
the impression that the tanks, though important, were not crucial to

success. The infantry were so instructed that they must not wait for a delayed tank and should a tank succeed, it must go to the aid of any infantry who found themselves held up. The tanks were tasked with crushing the barbed wire and engaging the enemy's machine-gun and rifle fire.

Against the wishes of Major General C. St L. Barter, commanding 47th (2nd London) Division, British troops already in High Wood were not withdrawn during the bombardment of the German-held areas of the wood. The opposing lines were both within the '100% zone' of the British artillery, leaving the gunners no choice but to lift the range to avoid hitting their infantry comrades and by doing so, many of the defending Germans went unscathed. This negative effect on the British troops was further exacerbated by the 100-yard wide corridors left free of artillery fire in order to improve the tanks' chances of not becoming victims of short shooting and at the same time, allowing the tanks to engage the enemy.

Yet another trap awaited the soldiers of 47th Division:

Secret – Issued with Fourth Army No. 209/17 (G) dated 11/9/16
  Instructions for the Employment of 'Tanks'
The stationary barrage of both heavy and field artillery will be timed to be lifted off the objectives of the tanks some minutes before their arrival at these objectives.

Due to the appalling ground conditions pertaining in High Wood, none of the four tanks that gained the interior of the wood reached their objectives and, given that the attack was timetable based, the artillery was absent when the infantry were most in need of its protection. This was not an oversight of the Army Staff; it was purely the result of the lack of a reliable means of communication between the front lines and the gunners, a condition that afflicted all the belligerents during the First World War.

Great things were expected of the new tanks but some officers were aware of the machines' agonisingly slow speed of ten-fifteen yards per minute over bad ground. In the case of High Wood, the divisional and tank officers had argued unsuccessfully for the tanks to move around the edges of the wood to avoid the tangle of roots and tree stumps which could bring them to a halt. In this they were overruled by III Corps

Commander, General Pulteney. Had the views of division and tank personnel prevailed, there would have been no need of the 100-yard wide, shell-free corridor or the time tabled lifting off the target.

The most distant objective for the tanks involved an advance of up to 1,859 yards in a north-easterly direction taking in the German position known as the Cough Drop. Of interest to note, the tracks designated for the two right hand tanks would take them through the High Wood mine craters, not around them.

Some, and by no means all, of the orders/instructions relating to the first ever use of the new weapon in battle conditions are quoted below.

In orders issued to 140 Brigade (Brigadier General Thomas Walter Brand, (3rd Viscount Hampden of Glynde) and 141 Brigade (Brigadier General Robert McDouall) would attack High Wood head on along the wood's southern face and also outflank the wood along the eastern and western faces. Attention was drawn to the lack of battle experience among the tank personnel alluded to in paragraph 14, b:

> *Tank officers are without exception strange to the ground and to the conditions of the battle. They will require a good deal of assistance from staffs of formations, particularly in the study of the ground over which the tanks will have to advance.*
>
> *Paragraph, c: Every Tank going into action should be provided with a map showing its track clearly marked, and the objectives of the infantry with time table.*

A four page appendix to the above orders stipulates in item (10):

> *After the capture of the most distant objectives Tanks will be withdrawn under Corps arrangements to previously selected positions some way in rear of these objectives. Arrangements must be made for replenishing the petrol and ammunition supply.*

Reading these hundred-year-old orders quickly leads to the conclusion that every eventuality had been covered, thus:

> *In the event of a Tank being left behind and having to follow the infantry, who have passed on, arrangements will be made, as far as possible, to ensure a party of two or three men being left to*

guide the Tank up to the objective and remove wounded men from in front of it.

General Rawlinson himself proposed 'use the tanks at night and come back before dawn and keep the Germans guessing.'

To modern eyes, these orders often appear wildly optimistic but the seeds of optimism can be traced to the 'stunts' of a compulsory nature performed by the tanks in the Army rear areas prior to deployment. Officers came away from these 'stunts' in the belief that the 26/27-ton tank could go anywhere and do anything, hence the exact timetables specified for the coming battle particularly in regard to the tank being in position in front of the infantry prior to Zero Hour. Senior planners had been led to believe that the tanks' petrol consumption gave a range of approximately 55 miles from the 46/50 gallons carried in the on-board fuel tanks. The reality though was brought home when Lieutenant Basil Henriques, commanding the tank C22 attached to 6th Division, discovered that his tank had consumed half of its fuel on the short but difficult approach to the jumping-off point; somehow Archie Holford-Walker, brother of Allen, managed to conjure up sixteen gallons of petrol at 2.30am with which to replenish C22, and this in a dangerous battle area.

When first conceived, the tank was seen as a throw away weapon having a life of 50 miles before being broken up for spares or scrap. At a cost of £5,000 (£215,300 at 2015 values) it soon became apparent that the machines would have to last much longer. One authority gives the running cost of an Mk I tank at £7 per mile, the equivalent of £301.42p at 2015 values.

The guns of Fourth Army had been firing since 12 September and as the sun rose over the ruined landscape of the Somme battlefield on 15 September 1916, the artillery roared forth its bellowing cacophony of defiance. A total of 1,064 guns and howitzers had already fired 828,000 shells, a considerable number, but just under half the number used for the 14 July attack over similar ground. In the case of High Wood, where the tanks were to provide 'mobile artillery', the dilution effect on the already thin barrage was multiplied.

The orders were for 140 Brigade to attack on 47th Division's right protecting the flank of the New Zealand Division and extending as far left as Sap 4. On 15 September at 12.03am the adjutant of the 6th (City of London) Battalion London Regiment synchronised the watches to be carried by officers making the attack. At 12.14am Second Lieutenant Jacobs did likewise for the watches used by the 8th (City of London) Battalion (Post Office Rifles). Problems were emerging, at 06.14am the adjutant of 1/15th (County of London) Battalion (Civil Service Rifles) reported *'one pair of tanks had lost direction and would be late.'* It is at this moment that a controversy was born; the Tank D13, 'Delilah' (a female), was reported to be at its start point at 04.20am ready to leave at 05.53am, twenty-seven minutes in front of the infantry. In the meantime, the tank's engine would be allowed to cool and any last minute adjustments made.

The Debut of the Tank

Infantry and tank co-operation was an unknown concept during the Somme fighting. As late as June 1917 just prior to the Battle of Messines, Lieutenant Charles Lander, whom we met in July 1916, was warned *'avoid tanks, they draw fire and go for their own objective.'* Although the tanks achieved much at the Battle of Cambrai in November 1917, co-operation between the two arms was by no means universal. June 1918 heralded a more advanced method of applying the two arms together to produce success. The night time raid by five female tanks and the King's Own Yorkshire Light Infantry near the village of Bucquoy (7 miles west by north of Bapaume) on 22/23 June 1918, proved a great success.

On 4 July at the Battle of Hamel the Australians pulled off a lighting coup in co-operation with their previously hated tanks. It was on record that a tank could absorb the same amount of machine-gun fire that would have stalled an entire division of infantry. On 15 September 1916 the female Tank D24 successfully reached the outskirts of Martinpuich and in doing so destroyed three machine guns; had these guns been left undisturbed they would have undoubtedly wreaked havoc on the attacking British troops. As D.G. Brown noted in his book, *The Tank in Action during the First World War: 'iron mechanically moved saves blood, the tank is an economiser of life.'*

Delilah's commander, Lieutenant Sampson, was somewhat surprised to be informed that the infantry were moving off at 5.50am, before it became light enough for the enemy to observe troop movements.

Sampson's tank was left behind by the infantry and upon entering High Wood a little after 6am soon found herself the target for every German who could shoot or throw something. The tank was lurching violently, buffeting the crew in all directions, molten lead from bullet strikes began to penetrate small crevices in the hull plates, and by now the temperature inside the tank would have reached 120°F. But Delilah pressed on engaging the enemy with a murderous fire during which commotion a tree stump lifted a sponson door off its hinges, exposing the crew to the rain of death hissing through the wood. In an act of supreme bravery Gunner Chandler promptly exited the tank and re-fitted the door before squeezing himself back through the 25x16 inch doorway.

Possibly Delilah stranded in High Wood.

Unfortunately the attacking infantry had been held up due to the unsuppressed German fire. Nevertheless, Delilah crossed the first enemy trench and had the next line in her sights when her over-stretched engine began to show distinct signs of distress: loss of power and backfiring. The only solution was to remove and clean all six spark plugs. With the tank stopped and frantic efforts to attend to the problem in hand, the German gunners lost no time in acquiring the range. The shells crept ever closer before one struck somewhere on the rear of the tank; the final impetus that convinced the crew to abandon the machine occurred when another shell passed clean through the tank. All eight of the crew escaped from the now burning tank to take shelter in a trench in High Wood that happened to contain seventy-five Germans who wished to surrender.

It was at this moment that a party of British soldiers arrived and laid claim to the prisoners; following negotiations, Delilah's crew were allotted fifteen of the total. The British soldiers were most likely to have been members of 140 Brigade, who had been out in no man's land early and had romped forward despite heavy machine-gun fire and reached the Switch Line on the eastern side of the wood. The timings of the above remain obscure.

Delilah's engine problems: MKs I to IV British heavy tanks employed the 105hp Daimler *motor* (as described in maker's handbook). A civilian product and excellent for that role, however, the motor was the only type available 'off the shelf' and in the numbers required for the early tanks. In civilian use the motor was only guaranteed for six months and required constant maintenance, some tasks stipulated to be carried out at six hourly intervals with the engine running. We can only imagine the tank crews' response to orders not to thrash the motor and to pull up when the six hourly checks were due. The game of life or the alternative of coming to a very sticky end did not allow of such luxuries.

By the time of the official Zero at 06.20am the hundreds of men of 140/141 Brigades were already in serious trouble, no man's land being in many places no more than 50 yards wide with the enemy on full alert and untouched by the barrage. Dawn of the new day brought death in many forms to the Londoners. Their enemies had not been suppressed or driven off by the artillery, the tanks had failed to arrive, leaving the unfortunate infantry to face bullets, grenades, high explosive and shrapnel shells. They were cut to pieces. High Wood was living up to its name as 'The Rottenest Place on the Somme'.

Two tanks, D21 and D22 should have departed the southern corner of High Wood at 05.51am to proceed to a point inside the wood, just left of the mine crater to arrive at 06.19am – a journey of 350 yards. The two tanks departed late and made very slow progress until 06.30am when D21 fell into a British trench in the wood recorded as S4c 8.2 and broke a track, rendering the machine helpless. D22 was observed crashing its way through the wood by infantry ensconced in Anderson Trench. At 06.45am the tank suddenly veered right before reaching the crater, straddling Worcester Trench where it abutted Anderson Trench and became stuck.

C23 stranded in High Wood.

Tragedy, which had been waiting in the wings, now struck; believing themselves to be over a German-held trench the crew opened fire on the occupants not knowing that their 'enemies' were in fact members of 1/6th London (City of London Rifles). A heated verbal exchange is said to have taken place before the tank ceased fire; the number of killed and wounded in this incident was not recorded but at the same time soldiers of 1/8th Londons (Post Office Rifles) who were waiting to 'go over the top' were caught in a bombardment when the Germans spotted D22.

The final tank of the four to enter High Wood, C23 (a male), had a longer approach march than the D Company tanks, causing the crew to be extremely tired even before going into action. Under the command of Lieutenant Henderson, C23 was behind time when she entered High Wood and after travelling only 50 yards the tank became ditched in a British trench. The young commander informed his HQ by means of his carrier pigeon that he was *'hopelessly stuck'*. The tank did stay in action, however, firing its 6-pounders and machine guns. C23 was close by on the left of Delilah causing concern to Lieutenant Sampson that his tank was soon to be destroyed by the enthusiastic gunners of C23. Sampson left his tank in order to enquire as to the nature of C23's endeavours. Henderson's replied that he was *'laying a protective barrage'*, which as we have previously noted, is exactly what he was present in High Wood to do. This incident must have taken place when Delilah was still in

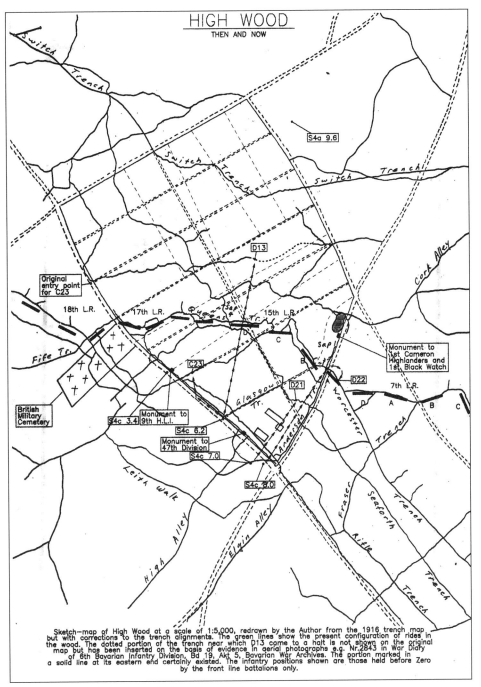

Final position of the tanks in High Wood. (Trevor Pidgeon – Permission of Pen & Sword)

action as we know that her crew made a quick exit following the failure of her engine and, in fact, Delilah came to a stop when she was 300 yards from C23; a round trip of 600 yards that Sampson would have been most unlikely to survive. C23 was badly damaged by artillery at 11.40am, she also had the distinction of being the last tank to leave High Wood. She was not removed until after the Second World War, further, she also appeared in a painting of High Wood commissioned by the British Government.

The type of terrain experienced by the pioneering/inexperienced tank crews has been well described by Alan Maude, editor of the *History of the 47th Division*:

> *Imagine Hampstead Heath made of cocoa-powder, and the natural surface folds further complicated by countless shell holes, each deep enough to hold a man and everywhere meandering crevices where men live below the surface of the ground, and you will get some idea of the terrain of the attack. The absence of natural landmarks must always be borne in mind, for it explains what might seem to be instances of confusion and bad map-reading in the process of operations.*

How went the day for the infantry?
We have seen above that except for elements of 140 Brigade (who, despite success, had suffered heavy casualties) the infantry were in trouble. Fortunately for history, the war diary of 140 Brigade has survived and its terse, one line entries, allows today's readers to follow the course of the battle minute by minute.

15 September 1916
B6.20am: *Zero (there is no mention of amended time for Zero)*
   6.33am *Artillery O.P. [Observation Post] reported that they have seen the NEW ZEALANDERS advancing.*
   6.50am *Adjutant 15/Battalion reported on telephone that a runner had reported that they had taken the front line.*
   7.05am *Adjutant 15/Battalion reported first Line taken. 2nd, 3rd, and 4th waves have passed over on their way to objective. Wounded Corporal returned who reports that he received his wound in Switch Line.*

7.24am 15/Battalion reported that they had heard that 17/Battalion (Poplar and Stepney Rifles) and 18/Battalion (London Irish Rifles) are held up in German front line.

7.30am (about) 6/Battalion (City of London) report they are being heavily shelled. 7/Battalion (City of London) report objective gained. 23 German prisoners arrive.

7.45am Received from 7/Battalion, they have occupied their objective with comparatively little loss.

7.49am 8/Battalion report left being hung up, but right has pushed on.

7.59am 47th Division informs us verbally that aeroplane reports red flares at S.5.d.4.9 & S.5.d.3.7-S.4.a.1.3. [These references show that British troops appeared to be in occupation of the Switch Line in High Wood and part of its continuation east of the Wood.]

8.29am Lieutenant Wallis arrived and reported that the New Zealanders had informed him at 8.a.m. that they had taken 2nd objective.

8.40am Orders to 15/Battalion telling them to try and get in touch with 7/Battalion in Switch Line. [This was to avoid gaps in the line that could be infiltrated by the enemy.]

9.15am Received from Division (47th) 1 battalion of 142 Brigade to move up.

As a point of interest, 142 Brigade orders stipulated that *'officers will carry no public money'*; this brigade also called for: *'Torn up paper on principle of paper chase will be utilised by assaulting troops to indicate routes for runners, wounded etc.'*

Note that once again intelligence desperately needed to conduct the battle has to rely on 'a wounded corporal', second hand telephone reports and runners guided by pieces of torn up paper. The use of red flares noted above could only work if the troops carrying them had survived thus far and the flare was noticed by an observer with the means to communicate. Follow-up waves were advancing but most of the troops ran into their fellows who were held up by the violence of the opposition. The unprotected troops were going down in large numbers and unless a quick, radical solution could be found those same troops faced annihilation.

The 1/17th London (Poplar and Stepney Rifles, 1/18th London (London Irish Rifles) and half of 1/15th London (Civil Service Rifles) had to fight for every inch of ground as the German defenders threw everything at the attackers, coupled with machine-gun fire from concrete emplacements that had not been destroyed. A follow-up wave of Londoners consisting of 19th, 20th, and elements of 8th Battalion joined their comrades in the desperate struggle for the wood. No less than five battalions of Londoners were now engaged in the most dangerous onslaught, although as the tide bypasses a rock, British troops were gaining ground along the east and west sides of the wood, and if enough men survived, they would soon find themselves in a position from which they would be able to enfilade the German defenders.

Meanwhile, the troops engaged in the frontal assault were faced with the very real possibility of failure. In a heroic attempt to revitalise the attack, 32-year-old Lieutenant Colonel, A.P. Hamilton, 1/19th London (St Pancras) called for all available men around his HQ to follow him up to High Wood; along with many others, the gallant colonel lost his life in the endeavour. Men of the 1/8th (Post Office Rifles) were trapped in shell holes; they could neither advance nor retreat without meeting their maker. Bravery there was in abundance that morning in High Wood; the officers who pushed forward paid with their lives, Captains Webb, Chichester, Mitchell and Lieutenant Kennedy were all killed, along with large numbers of their men. Later examination of High Wood revealed lines of dead British soldiers lying shoulder to shoulder on the edge of the mine crater.

The grave of Lieutenant Colonel Arthur Percival Hamilton.

History has bequeathed to us the details of the demise of Captain Webb (Post Office Rifles) thanks to John Hamblin of Lancing College in Sussex where Harold Oswald Townshend Webb was educated:

During the Attack on High Wood, Rifleman 'Porky' Knight of 'A' Company had come under heavy fire and seen his Company Commander and two of his Lieutenants fall. As the survivors scattered, he ran to some fallen trees and took cover. The machine

Captain Harold Oswald Townshend Webb

Harold Oswald Townshend Webb was born in Melbourne, Australia in 1887 the son of Stephen and Adele Alma Albertina Webb. Much travelled, Harold was christened at Boulogne in 1889.

Educated at Lancing College, Sussex from 1902–1905, Harold left school to work as an accountant and later became a Freemason, his residence being 6, Alma Square St John's Wood, London.

July 1914 found Harold in Egypt where he married Maria (nee Parmigiani) at the British Consulate in Cairo.

When Harold enlisted as a private into the Royal Fusiliers (1st Public School) Battalion on 2 September 1914, his army medical records state that he was 5ft 8½in tall and weighed 11 stones. His meteoric promotion to sergeant was followed by Harold's request to return to the rank of private. However, a commission soon followed with him being appointed to 3/8th (County of London) Battalion in June 1915. Embarking for France on 28 December 1915, Harold was posted to 1/8th (Post Office Rifles) London Regiment.

Lancing College Memorial, Captain Webb is amongst those former pupils remembered here.

Lancing College Chapel.

At the time of his death (15 September 1916) Harold was 29 years old, leaving a widow and his daughter Violet who had been born on 21 September 1915. A visit to Lancing College Chapel is highly recommended, a fabulous building housing a magnificent memorial to former students who lost their lives in two World Wars.

The Webb family suffered further loss when in March 1918, another son, Stanley Jules Webb was killed while serving as a private with the East Yorkshire Regiment; Stanley is recorded on the Arras Memorial.

gun fire continued to be fierce and he glanced over his shoulder to see Captain Webb approaching from the rear with a revolver in his hand about 9am, Webb called out (in the words of the Duke of Wellington at Waterloo) "Up Knight and at them" and together they rushed the enemy machine gun post but Harold Webb was killed and 'Porky' was wounded in the right thigh.

In an example of one of those actions when junior ranks act on initiative; around 9am a young officer had left the interior of High Wood to seek out Captain Goodes who commanded 140 Brigade Trench Mortar Battery. Appraising Goodes of the situation, a fire plan was conceived in record time. By 9.30am Goodes and his men opened what proved to be a devastating fifteen-minute bombardment with their mortars. When 9.45am came the battery ceased fire having discharged 750 mortar bombs into the previously unhindered enemy-held section of the wood.

140 Brigade, 10.13am Captain Goodes reported that his mortars had fired 750 rounds of Stokes (mortar bombs) into the German line in ¼ of an hour.

11.20am Germans reported surrendering in batches in High Wood.

Following the first signs of German mass surrender, another of High Wood's long list of tragedies played out. Major J.R. Trinder 1/18th London (London Irish Rifles) was supervising the removal of German prisoners to the rear. While engaged in this act of getting former enemies to safety, he was shot through the head by one of the still-active snipers. What advantage was there to the enemy for the killing of this 25 year old? Would the course of the war be altered in favour of Germany? No. Would it have endangered the lives of the captured former comrades of the sniper? Yes, it could very well have done so. Major Trinder is buried in Flat Iron Copse Cemetery, Plot V111. Row 1 grave 2.

12.25pm *Officer Commanding 15/Battalion reports HIGH WOOD in our possession, estimates casualties 50%, including three Company Commanders.*

12.37pm 140 Brigade reports – HIGH WOOD in our hands.

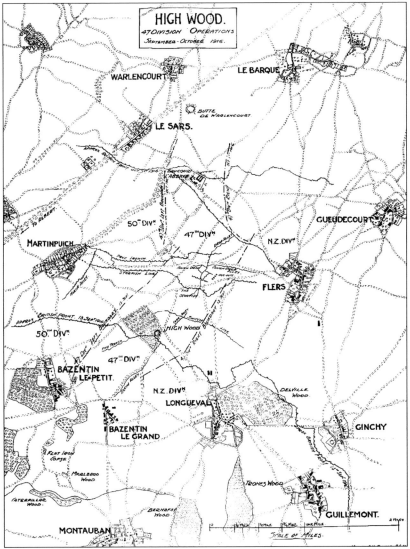

47th Division operational area also shows 50th and New Zealand Divisions in action either side of High Wood.

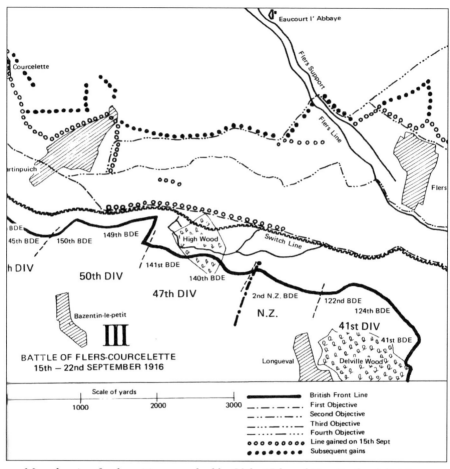

Scale of yards

1000	2000	3000	

British Front Line
First Objective
Second Objective
Third Objective
Fourth Objective
Line gained on 15th Sept
Subsequent gains

Map showing final positions reached by 50th, 47th and New Zealand divisions on 15 September.

The war diary of 47th Division for 15 September makes little mention of the capture of High Wood, but the prime purpose of war diaries was not to celebrate captures but to record the attaining or not of objectives set for that particular formation. High Wood, for all its evil reputation was merely an obstacle to the objectives of the Switch Line and beyond that the Starfish Line. The part played in the taking of High Wood by Captain Goodes and his team was well described when a Captain Deverell, Post Office Rifles, wrote:

> *As you know High Wood was our objective, and our Trench Mortar Batteries under jolly old Goodes really saved the situation, as the Tanks were not worth a d—-n there and never did anything but spoil the show. The Boche was not touched*

there (High Wood) when the attack took place, and it was hung up until Goodes had done wonderful work with his guns. Then things went alright.

Success on the Western Front could never be achieved in isolation, the wider the attack frontage then the less likely it was that enemy forces could turn the flanks of the attackers and thereby subject the attacking forces to enfilade fire. In the case of 47th Division on 15 September, 50th (Northumbrian) Division would attack on the Londoners' left and their right-hand neighbours would be the New Zealand Division. Meanwhile the 50th Division (Major General P.S. Wilkinson), with two brigades in the line, was tasked to take Prue Trench (east of Martinpuich and half a mile north of High Wood) and Martinpuich.

The 50th Division started well forward of their neighbours in the hope that this would render assistance to 47th Division. All went well until the advance on the Starfish Line and the Bow commenced; enfilade fire began to pour from High Wood into the attacking waves of the north-countrymen. At 8.10am 4th Northumberland Fusiliers began a bombing attack towards High Wood in an attempt to assist 47th Division, as the enemy was seen to be emerging from the wood in a likely attempt to outflank the Londoners. Losses among the north-countrymen were high as heavy fighting took place north-west of High Wood where the 6th Northumberland Fusiliers eventually established a defensive flank.

Meanwhile, the New Zealand Division attacked on the right of 47th Division on a 900-yard front. The Kiwis jumping-off position can be traced today as it coincided with what is now the rear wall of Caterpillar Valley Cemetery. By 6am all the attacking troops of the division had

High Wood from Caterpillar Valley Cemetery showing much of the ground fought over on 15 September.

consumed breakfast accompanied by rum. Forward movement commenced 30 seconds before zero with the grim prospect for the troops of advancing down an open slope prior to attacking uphill to engage the enemy ensconced in the Switch Line. 'Leaning' too heavily on the barrage, which moved at 54 yards per minute, caused casualties among the Kiwis, as did the ever-present menace of machine-gun fire from High Wood. But in a remarkable advance of thirty minutes duration, and a ferocious hand-to-hand fight, the division was in possession of their portion of the previously impregnable Switch Line at 6.50am.

High Wood had now become untenable for the German defenders as both the 47th and New Zealand divisions were in a position to outflank the wood and cut off the enemy garrison who had endured the onslaught of the Stokes mortar bombardment by 47th Division. General Harper (51st Division) was once heard to quantify outflanking the enemy as: *'Not just shooting through the side windows but getting into the rear and kicking the back door in'.*

After two months and one day of fighting, the battle was closed down at 3pm and, as darkness fell and rain began to fall, so ended the deadly struggle for High Wood, now reduced to forty bare poles and a map reference inhabited by ghosts, rats and flies.

Aftermath

The 47th Division's losses at High Wood numbered something over 4,500 killed, wounded, or missing. Following two whole months of failed attempts, the Londoners – with the noble contribution of their neighbouring divisions – had triumphed. Rumblings began almost immediately the wood was taken: the price was too high, someone had to be sacrificed and the search for a scapegoat began. The axe fell on Major General Charles C. Barter. Although 47th Division had undoubtedly won through on 15 September, General Barter was dismissed on 19 September by Lieutenant General W.P. Pulteney, commander of III Corps for *'wanton waste of life*, a charge vigorously denied by Barter for the remainder of his life; he died while resident in Madrid in 1931. It is interesting to note that history can give different versions of the same event. Sir Douglas Haig wrote:

> *The 47th Div. failed at High Wood on 15 September and the GOC was sent home! Barter by name, now Gorringe has taken over command.*

'Forty bare poles' High Wood, photographed by Charles Fair in 1920.

The person Haig refers to was Lieutenant General Sir George Frederick Gorringe (1868-1945) who commanded the 47th for the remainder of the war.

History has bequeathed to us the letters and memoirs of Major Charles Fair of the 19th London Regiment (St Pancras), Major Fair had attended Pembroke College, Cambridge, where he gained a first class honours in classics. A prolific and descriptive letter writer, his communications have become invaluable to history. Major Fair assumed command of the battalion following the death in action at High Wood of his commanding officer Lieutenant Colonel Hamilton. The major tells of his sadness at the loss of

Charles Fair.

so many friends and comrades on 15 September, including three company commanders, the regimental sergeant major, a company sergeant major and his own servant. In a letter to his father dated 24 September Major Fair writes:

> *Dear Dad,*
> *Everyone seems enormously proud of what the Brigade (141) and our Battalion (1/19 (St. Pancras)) has accomplished. At any rate we did what many others failed to do and took a place which has cost many thousands of casualties and which is the last of the really high ground which the Germans occupied in this part of the world. We had a pretty rough time and lost many of our best.*

The bodies of these unfortunate men referred to by Major Fair, became the nucleus of what is now the London Cemetery opposite High Wood. Major Fair corresponded with General Edmunds, the British Official Historian and on 15 May 1935, wrote:

> *In all the period of well over two years which I spent with an infantry battalion in France and Belgium, I never saw such gruesome scenes as in and around High Wood. I went round it with General McDouall on the morning of 16 September and it seemed that every infantry unit of both armies (German and British) was represented by the dead, some of whom had been lying there since 14 July.*

Survivors of the 19th Londoners found themselves engaged in the collection and burial of the dead, many of whom the burial parties must have known, leading the Chaplain of 47th Division, the Reverend D. Railton to note:

> *Many men, who have stood it all, cannot stand this clearing of the battlefield. This Battalion was left to do that, and several men went off with shell shock... caused not just by the explosion of a nearby shell, but by the sights and smell and horror of the battlefield in general. I felt dreadful, and had to do my best to keep the men up to the task.*

The Battle of the Somme would go on until mid-November but as early as 10 September, Ludendorff opined in a conversation with a naval officer that he had no faith in being able to force the war to a favourable conclusion by means of land forces. To succeed, Germany had no option but to employ unrestricted submarine warfare. Hindenburg also added his weight to the submarine policy declaring:

> *The German General Staff is bound to adopt unrestricted U-boat warfare as one of its measures, because among other things it will relieve the situation on the Somme front.*

By 16 September, Ludendorff had initiated plans for the German army in the west to take up a defensive role. The historian John Terraine notes in *Business in Great Waters* that the new defensive line some miles in the rear of the Somme battlefield gave Germany the options of making peace overtures while occupying someone else's country, planning a new offensive or using the opportunity to husband national resources in order to concentrate on unrestricted submarine warfare against Great Britain; she chose the last.

By 13 November, the forces of Great Britain and France had fought the mightiest army in the world to a standstill on the Somme. Germany was not yet beaten but she had paid a terrible price for her invasions, with more to come as the Somme set off the action of last resort via the unrestricted use of submarines. It ultimately caused the entry of the USA into the war and sealed the fate of Germany. As previously mentioned, in the words of Sun Tzu 'weapons are tools of ill omen...' We cannot live in the past but we can learn from it.

Chapter 5

'There Will Be Voices Whispering Down These Ways'

The above words by Geoffrey Winthrop Young in his poem 'Looking Forward' penned in the year 1909, strike a chord when visiting the former battlefields of France and Flanders, especially so when the visitor takes a quiet moment on the still rural Somme and in the national park of Verdun. It is possible to hear nought but the wind whispering in the leaves and branches of the woods and swishing through the fields of standing crops; equally poignant are the words of an anonymous writer, 'listen awhile you will hear them still'.

John Glubb (1897-1986) later Lieutenant General Sir John and commander of the Arab Legion, served as commander of a field company of Royal Engineers operating tramways in the High Wood area. During his service on the Western Front, Glubb sustained three wounds including a shattered jaw. His father was also serving on the Western Front as Commander Royal Engineers, Second Army. The author of several books, John Glubb's *Into Battle* is his memoir of his time on the Western Front from which we quote below.

High Wood tourism began early once the area had been made relatively safe, meaning that the British side of the ridge was no longer under observation by the enemy.

26th December 1916, High Wood is quite the place for a tourist now, with the following items of interest:
Two derelict tanks from 15th September
Crosses commemorating the 1st division and the 47th and our own Northumberland Fusiliers
Several very fine German deep dugouts and a concrete blockhouse
One of the finest views I ever saw, including nearly all the Somme battlefields and the present German front lines.

Very large quantities of unexploded ordnance still littered the battlefield and in some cases were hidden just below the surface, making the casual lighting of fires a very dangerous practice. The 7th Durham Light Infantry lost several men in this way when an explosion occurred following the lighting of a fire. The explosion took place in late December 1916 or early January 1917 when the battalion was in the Mametz Wood – High Wood area. (See *Eighth Battalion Durham Light Infantry* published circa 1926.)

January 1917 found John Glubb still in the area of High Wood, he describes the difficulties of coaxing the tiny petrol engine locomotives and their loads up the steep gradients to High Wood, making one mile per hour with sappers sanding the rails by hand to increase traction and infantry 'pushers' assisting at the rear. On the return trips down the slopes, the infantrymen indulged in the dangerous practice of sitting on the trucks and hurtling downhill at great speed. At least one man broke a leg as a result of the inevitable derailments. The officer in charge of the outer (High Wood) terminus became well known for his voluble stream of orders, advice and counter orders, occasioned upon the arrival of a ration train. So much so, that a later concert party portrayal of the officer 'brought the house down'.

A strange incident occurred in High Wood during the winter of 1917 and is recorded in Donald Boyd's book *Salute the Guns*; permission was given by Pen & Sword to quote from this excellent work. Two gunner officers had met up with a salvage company working near Bazentin-le-Grande and were told of an NCO who, when using field glasses, had spotted deserters in High Wood. They were spotted again the next evening, probably foraging for food. The following morning seven or eight deserters who were occupying dug-outs in High Wood surrendered to a party of NCOs and an officer. Others who made a fight of it were killed when grenades were thrown and the dug-outs collapsed. The officer also related how a mess cart had earlier been found devoid of the rations it had carried and minus the driver who was never found. This leaves us with an unanswered question; is there a driver recorded on the Thiepval Memorial to the Missing of the Somme who is actually a murder victim?

Once again we encounter Major Charles Fair as he undertakes *A Visit to Old Haunts*, the story of his pilgrimage to the scene of his experiences in the war. The journey was made in April 1920, just eighteen months

after the signing of the Armistice. The importance of Charles Fair's
account cannot be over estimated as he was 'there' during the battle and
returned long before memories began to fade and distort. We are told
that the village of Contalmaison could only be traced by three surviving
steps to the church. Only 'forty bare poles' remained of High Wood, but
the site of 141 Brigade's HQ was located and photographed with Charles
included. The party also traced the old German positions and marvelled
at the observation granted to the enemy while he held the wood.

Major Charles Fair, High Wood 1920.

Noting a group of graves 'outside the wood' Charles quickly realised that they contained the men he had known and lost on 15 September 1916. These men still lie today in what became plot one of the CWGC London Cemetery. Colonel Hamilton who is mentioned in Chapter Four is buried in Flat Iron Copse Cemetery, approximately 3,300 yards distant as the crow flies from High Wood.

Here follows a brief summary of the details of some of Major Fair's friends and colleagues who died on 15 September with information kindly provided by the Commonwealth War Graves Commission. In defiance of convention, a capital letter has been used by the present writer to denote Son or Husband; they were probably the most important people in the world to those they left behind. The full title of 19th London is (County of London) Battalion (St Pancras); for the sake of brevity the shortened version is used below. Additional information such as where born etc has been taken from 'Soldiers Died' a British Government publication of 1921 which itself was based on records supplied by individual regiments.

Company Serjeant Major George Bolton, 19th London, born Kentish Town, enlisted Camden Town, resident Tottenham. Serre Road Cemetery No.2, grave V.D.20.

Second Lieutenant Alfred Lynn Cooper, age 23, 19th London, Son of Mr and Mrs Cooper of 65, Barkston Gardens, Earls Court, London. London Cemetery, grave, 1A.A.9.

Captain Leigh Jacob Davis, age 24, 19th London, Son of Mr and Mrs Arthur Richard Davis of 11, Cleve Rd, West Hampstead, London. London Cemetery, grave 1A.A.15.

Lance Serjeant Arthur William Deighton, 19th London, born Clapton, enlisted Barnet, resident Stoke Newington. London Cemetery, grave 1A.D.5.

Captain Alexander George Gauld, age 23, 19th London, Son of Alexander and Isabella Gauld, of 24, Hornsey Lane, Highgate, London. London Cemetery, grave 1A.A.14.

Lieutenant Colonel Arthur Percival Hamilton, age 32, The Queen's (Royal West Surrey Regiment) attached to 19th London, Son of the late Major P.F.P. Hamilton, Royal Artillery and Mrs Hamilton, Husband of Kate G. Hamilton, of 42, Eaton Square, London. Flat Iron Copse Cemetery, grave Vll.1.2.

Captain David Henderson, age 27, 8th Middlesex (Duke of

Cambridge's Own) attached to 19th London, Son of the Right Honourable Arthur Henderson MP and of Eleanor Henderson (née Watson). London Cemetery, grave 1A.A.14.

Second Lieutenant Samuel Wilfred Pleydell-Bouverie, age 20, 19th London, Son of Mr and Mrs W. Pleydell-Bouverie, London Cemetery, grave 1A.A.1.

Private Frederick Prewer, age 21, A Company, 19th London, enlisted Camden Town, resident Kentish Town, Son of Mr And Mrs Frederick James Prewer of 22, Prince of Wales Crescent, St Pancras, London. London Cemetery, grave 1A.A.12.

Regimental Serjeant Major Arthur Frederick Ridout, 19th London, enlisted Camden Town, resident Tooting Junction, Son of Frederick and Elizabeth Ridout, of Okeford Fitzpaine, Dorsetshire, Husband of Ella Ridout, of 14, Balham Park Road, Balham, London. London Cemetery, grave 1A. A.11.

Second Lieutenant Tom Hollingworth Rowson, age 27, 19th London, Son of Mr and Mrs J.W. Rowson of Bridport, Dorsetshire, Husband of Dorothy C. Rowson, of 11 Knights Hill, West Norwood, London. London Cemetery, grave 1A.A.17.

Lance Corporal Edward Thomas Toole, 19th London, born St Pancras, enlisted Camden Town, resident Drummond Street. London Cemetery, grave. 1A.D.2.

Private Arthur George Whybrow, age 23, 19th London, enlisted Camden Town, resident Kentish Town, Son of John and Louisa Whybrow, of Hampstead, London, Husband of Daisy Whybrow, of 193, Junction Road, Highgate, London. London Cemetery, grave 1A.A.10.

The original 47th Division Memorial situated on the D107 road was unveiled in 1925 by Major General Sir William Thwaites; it is not known if Charles Barter was present. The present memorial was erected and

47th Division Memorial Garden, Martinpuich.

dedicated in 1996 due to the original being affected by subsidence. In nearby Martinpuich, the school, loggia and attached playground were provided by the 47th Division. The architect of both was W.G. Newton, who had fought at High Wood and been awarded the Military Cross for action therein.

Another class of 'tourist' arrived following the fall of France in 1940. The Mathon family told a long dead friend of the present writer that a party of German soldiers arrived in 1940 expressing a desire to visit High Wood; unable to refuse, Monsieur Mathon could only advise that the wood held unexploded ordnance and to be very careful. Shortly afterwards a loud explosion was heard which the family subsequently discovered had resulted in the deaths of two of the visiting Germans.

Original 47th Division Memorial at High Wood (Charles Fair 1920).

Don Price, ex Public Schools Battalion, 20th Royal Fusiliers planted an oak tree in High Wood 10 yards west of the 47th Division Memorial on 3 May 1987. Mr Price believed that he was one of the last men alive to have fought in the Wood. The tree still flourishes.

Mention should be made of the Royal British Legion pilgrimage to the Western Front which took place in August 1928 allowing 10,000 ex-servicemen or widows of those killed to visit the area. Beaucourt Station situated on the Somme battlefield and fairly close to the new Newfoundland Park was chosen as the point of disembarkation. Over 5,000 pilgrims arrived at Beaucourt on 7/8 August and many wished to travel to points further afield than those within walking distance of the station. High Wood would be included in the more distant destinations located as it is approximately 4.35 miles as the crow flies south-east of Beaucourt Station. Cars were laid on for the 'special visits', as they were known, but of the very few such visits recorded in the souvenir book of the whole pilgrimage, no mention is made of High Wood. However, given the sinister reputation of High Wood and its surrounding area it would be highly probable that visits did take place. The group of pilgrims shown in the photograph are visiting Newfoundland Park,

Beaucourt Station.

1928 Pilgrims at Newfoundland Park.

Human remains in the 'Bloody Road' illustrating the difficulty of identifying remains. May he rest in peace.

notice that they do not seem in the least gloomy, and have no problems examining the rifles and helmets that were scattered about in those days.

Post Battle Burial of the Dead

The post battle clearance and respectful interment of the dead became a major problem for all the combatants. In the white heat of battle nothing could be done for a fallen comrade, hastily covered bodies were likely to be blown out of their resting places and dismembered by exploding shells. The fighting infantry took an extreme dislike to the burial of their own and it was not until March 1915 that a Graves Registration Commission was formally established which in turn, became the Directorate of Graves Registration and Enquiries (DGRE) in February 1916.

The problem of identifying and burial of the dead continued long after the DGRE began its work. John Glubb became severely distressed by the sight of dead soldiers being devoured by millions of bluebottles following the capture of High Wood. Major Watson of the Heavy Branch Machine Gun Corps (later to become the Tank Corps) had occasion to cross the Somme battlefield by car in March 1917, four months after the fighting had ceased. He was greatly disturbed by the corpses still tangled in the barbed wire who seemed to be waving at him; it was actually the effect of the wind moving the limbs of the long dead unfortunates. The major went on to comment in his memoir *A Company of Tanks* (London 1920):

> *Our progress was slow. Soon we lit the lamps. The track was full of horrible shadows, and big dark things seemed to come down to the road to meet us. On either side of the car was the desert of mud or water-logged holes and corpses face downward under water. Everywhere maimed ghosts were rustling and plump rats were pattering along the trenches. It is unwise to go through a battlefield at night. If they make the Somme a forest, no man will be brave enough to cross it in the dark.*

A rather more robust view of the problem was taken by Lieutenant Colonel Fraser-Tytler in his memoir, *Field Guns in France* (circa 1922):

> *The 'Body Snatcher' or 'Cold Meat Specialist' (Corps Burial Officer) was most useful in removing our pet aversions, (corpses) which otherwise might have remained unburied for months.*

Soldiers on leave were telling of the masses of unburied bodies and in London the War Office began to receive letters from members of the public insisting that matters regarding the dead should be taken in hand urgently. The work did proceed, but the nature of the task defies description, we can only pass on to our readers the words of Private J. McCauley, who was allotted the ghastly duty:

> *Often I have picked up the remains of a fine brave man on a shovel, just a little heap of bones and maggots to be carried to the common burial place. Bodies were found submerged in the water filled shell holes and mine craters; bodies that seemed whole but became like huge masses of white, slimy chalk when we handled them. I shuddered as my hands, covered in soft flesh and slime, moved in search of the disc, and I have pulled bodies to pieces in order that they should not be buried unknown. It was very painful to have to bury the unknown.*

Thanks to Peter Hodgkinson, author of *Clearing the Dead* for the above quotation.

The words of Private McCauley are quite staggering, even more so when it is taken into account that at some time he had to return to a 'normal' life. That the vast majority of ex soldiers did re-adjust to civilian life can only be attributed in no small part to the great inner strength of that fine generation.

Exhumation in the post war period

Ernest Brookes, a man who stayed behind, provided this short account of his post war service searching for the 'missing' on the former battlefields. The author met and spoke with Ernest on several occasions in the early 1970s. He had served as a despatch rider and on one of his forays near the front, a small calibre shell had passed clean through the rear wheel of his motor cycle. This and many other similar scrapes, and his love of speed led to Ernest being awarded the title of 'Mad Brookes'. During our last conversation, Ernest related his experiences searching for the remains of the missing of the war. He volunteered for a Battlefields Exhumation Company at the rate of 2/6d per day. Unfortunately for history, the companies did not keep diaries of their movements, only maps with numbers of bodies recovered.

Ernest Brookes, battlefield searcher.

Ernest had stayed behind due to his belief that over a million fit young men would be scrambling for work in the post war UK, and knowing how he had gone short of food and other necessities of life prior to the war, Ernest had no desire to return to such a precarious situation. Food in plenty, drink, clothing and medical care would all have been sacrificed if Ernest had joined the civilian job seekers. So it was that Ernest found himself as a member of an Exhumation Company, which included a Survey Officer and Burial Officer. Each company was divided into squads of thirty-two men equipped with two pairs of rubber gloves, two shovels, stakes to mark the location of any graves found, rope and canvas with which the remains recovered could be secured for removal by stretcher, at least two pairs of wire cutters and finally 'Cresol', the trade name for a disinfectant/antiseptic liquid. Ernest recalled being dropped off from a 3-ton lorry in a moonscape where all landmarks had been swept away by the long artillery duels of the war. The men were provided with a handcart loaded with tools plus ample supplies of food and drink.

The accompanying photograph depicts Ernest sitting atop a stranded tank (circa 1920) just outside the Belgian city of Ypres; his experiences in the Ypres Salient would have been much the same on any part of the former Western Front. We know that the Somme was searched six times in this way and it is quite possible that Ernest was there. When asked how he could face food after dealing with corpses in advanced stages of decay, he replied, 'I didn't eat for the first three days but after that, I was so hungry I'd eat anything and it never bothered me again.'

Ernest's gang appear to have been very experienced in the art of searching their allotted squares of the battlefield; discoloured grass and water were often tell tale signs of the presence of a corpse. Upon reading these signs the gang pushed thin steel bars into the churned up ground sniffing the steel as it was removed; according to Ernest, this procedure gave proof enough to start the exhumation process. He also mentioned that chicken wire was used to wrap the body for removal to a cemetery which accords with reports that the canvas normally used for this purpose was in short supply. There were nervous breakdowns and others who became addicted to alcohol, but the clearing of the Western Front was not unique; it has existed in all wars down to the present day. Robert Braithwaite writing in *Afgantsy* (London, 2011) on the Russian experience in Afghanistan tells much the same story in regard to the men charged with preparing the dead to be sent home to Russia. We are fortunate that Ernest Brookes gave us a snapshot in time of post battle life 100 years ago.

The Lost Soldiers of High Wood

Just how many bodies of soldiers killed in High Wood were never recovered? Figures given from various sources range from 8,000 to 10,000 and the inevitable controversy rumbles on. Quoted below are actual records compiled by the exhumation companies that had worked in High Wood. The heart of High Wood is represented by trench map 'Longueval, Edition 2. E' square 4 and sub squares, a, b, c, and d.

Sub Square 4a: 89 nine bodies were recovered only one of which was positively identified being:
Private Frederick James Wood, 5958, 20th Royal Fusiliers, KIA 20 July 1916, aged 21. Two further bodies were partially identified in 4a 7.3 being 'Kenworthy and Lisbowman', nothing further is known at the time of writing.
Sub Square 4b: 80 bodies were recovered nine of which were positively identified being:
Private Joseph Birchfield, 5731, 7th London Regiment, KIA 18 September 1916.

Rifleman Thomas D. Cox, 3080, 17th London Regiment, KIA 1 October 1916.

Private Thomas W. Clough, 33651, 22nd Manchester Regiment, KIA 15 July 1916, aged 29.

Corporal William Mellis, 265357, Black Watch, KIA 30 July 1916, aged 26.

Rifleman Arthur Hipkiss, 3588, 2nd King's Royal Rifle Corps, KIA 9 September 1916, aged 35.

Rifleman Harry Hoyle, R/19972, King's Royal Rifle Corps, KIA 9 September 1916, aged 25.

Private Horace Marshall, 200756, 4th Cameron Highlanders, KIA 3 September 1916, aged 21.

Rifleman Harry Daykin, R/12411, 2nd King's Royal Rifle Corps, KIA 9 September 1916.

Private Richard Charles Wooden, G/14833, 2nd Royal Sussex, KIA 9 September 1916, aged 35.

Sub Square 4c: 661 bodies recovered of which 16 were positively identified being:

Private Edwin Henry Streatfield, G/12173, 1st Royal West Kents, KIA 22 July 1916, aged 25.

Private William Haycock, 6115, 1st South Staffordshires, KIA 10 July 1916, aged 37.

Corporal Thomas Henry Greenhalgh, 102871, 178 Tunnel Company, Royal Engineers, KIA 27 August 1916.

Rifleman George Raymond Dowson, C/1436, 6th King's Royal Rifle Corps, KIA 15 July 1916, aged 24.

Rifleman E. Wheatley, C/1229, 16 King's Royal Rifle Corps, KIA 15 July 1916, aged 19.

Rifleman Tom Howe, C/429, 16 King's Royal Rifle Corps, KIA 16 July 1916.

Rifleman Harry Pearce, C/634 16 King's Royal Rifle Corps, KIA 15 July 1916.

Major Adrian Deighton Cooban, 16 King's Royal Rifle Corps, KIA 16 July 1916, age 34.

Rifleman Harry Davey, 5775, 21st London Regiment, KIA 12 August 1916.

Private Herbert Warner, 17044, 2nd Machine Gun Corps, KIA 9 September 1916.

Private Ralph Fernando Morton, 8849, 20th Royal Fusiliers, KIA 20 July 1916.

Corporal Cecil Worthington, 5971, 20th Royal Fusiliers, KIA 20 July 1916, aged 33.

Lance Corporal L.J. Urquhart, 7035, D Company Scottish Rifles, KIA 20 July 1916, aged 19.

Gould, Private, Edward Francis, 7846, D Company, 20/Royal Fusiliers, KIA 20 July 1916, aged 32.

Private George Alan Bradley, GS/8878, Royal Fusiliers, KIA 20 July 1916, aged 19.

Serjeant Ernest Williamson, 5943, 20th Royal Fusiliers, KIA 20 July 1916

Sub Square 4d:
Private Bert William Inskip, G/14547, C Company 2nd Royal Sussex, KIA 9 September 1916, aged 19.

All of the above listed servicemen are buried in Caterpillar Valley Cemetery. Note the huge discrepancy between bodies found in 4c and 4d, it should be borne in mind that ground conditions in High Wood were chaotic; the thousands of trees that originally made up the wood had been reduced to forty shattered stumps. The rest of the trees were still there in some form or other from splintered trunks to kindling. Collapsed dugouts, shell holes, old trenches, miles of rusty barbed wire and large amounts of unexploded ordnance would have confronted the searchers. It must be concluded that the men of the Exhumation Companies did their best, but they were not forensic pathologists, as noted above in 4a, names appear that do not correlate to published records of the recovered dead of High Wood. At some time a bold historian will complete a dissertation on the dead and missing of the three national armies that fought in High Wood: a formidable task that would be a service to history.

The Last Word
High Wood with her seventy-five acres of now mature trees makes a magnificent sight for the weary traveller, she has outlived all who knew her in any capacity during the First World War; the armies have long departed the field leaving the khaki and field grey clad ghosts to sleep well in her shaded glades. She sits today guardian of her hilltop as she has always done and will do so long after we mortals have left this Earth behind.

Pax Vobiscum

Visiting the Battlefield

Beware of Battlefield Debris!

Beware, the shell and Stokes mortar round on the next page have been fired and failed to explode (technically a 'blind'). Do not disturb under any circumstances! Further, do not handle or allow any other person in your party to handle or in any way interfere with ammunition which may be encountered on the battlefield. Even clods of earth can conceal a hand grenade; be aware, keep to marked paths and stay safe.

Medical insurance is advisable. If taking your car carry spare bulbs, first aid kit, fire extinguisher, yellow jacket, warning triangle, observe speed limits and note, the drink-driving limit is half that of the UK. Carry clothing and footwear to cater for the capricious weather on the Somme; we have witnessed horizontal rain on several occasions and breathed air so hot in September that it parched our throats; the opposite can also be true and all in the same day.

The Somme battlefield is crisscrossed by green roads (tracks) and paths which are ideal for the walker. Please do not walk among growing crops or newly ploughed fields; the Somme is a working landscape in which we are guests. Do not leave vehicles unattended on green roads; they are used by large agricultural machines which, due to their size, cannot pass a parked vehicle.

High Wood is private property (as are many of the Somme woods) and should be treated as such.

Beware of hunting parties which run from approximately the middle of August to February/March. Do not cross gun lines or, for any reason whatsoever, enter woodland during the hunting season.

To all who visit the Somme, remember this is hallowed ground, the fields and woods still contain the unrecovered remains of thousands of soldiers from the armies of Great Britain and her Empire, the Commonwealth, France and Germany.

Never Forget.

Battlefield debris.

Where to stay
The Somme offers a wide range of accommodation from hotel chains to small family run establishments, a selection of both is listed below:

> *The Royal Picardie, Route d Amiens, 80300 Albert; Tel +33 322 75 01 64*
> *Hotel de la Basilique, 3-5 Rue Gambetta, 80300 Albert; Tel +33 322 75 08 11*

Auchonvillers, a small village located in the heart of the former battlefield where the visitor can stay with *Avril Williams at 10 Rue de Lattre, Auchonvillers, Tel +33 322 76 23 66*. Avril provides a full range of meals plus a bar. The site also contains an excellent museum dedicated to the Battle of the Somme and most certainly deserves public support.

MainVisitor Sites
Newfoundland Memorial Park, Beaumont Hamel, preserved First World War battlefield.
  The Ulster Tower (closed Mondays) near Thiepval on D73, provides a true Ulster welcome with drinks and sandwiches available. Very high quality tours of Thiepval Wood are offered twice daily, during which history does come to life. Tel +33 (0) 3 22 74 81 11
  Thiepval Memorial and Visitor Centre, Edwin Lutyens enormous memorial to the missing of the Somme stands in an area steeped in the history of the battle. The visitor centre is attached to the site and offers the use of computer databases to trace fallen soldiers; a wide range of books and maps are for sale, drinks machines and toilets are provided.
  South African Memorial and Museum at Delville Wood, the museum is open from 10am to 6pm Tuesday to Sunday. There is parking available on site together with toilets.

Remembrement:
Refers to a legal process carried out every thirty to forty years by which land is re-apportioned to prevent the build up of small plots of land which one owner may have scattered over a wide area. Following Remembrement, tracks may disappear while new ones come into use.

Thiepval Memorial to the Missing of the Somme.

Battlefield Tours
By vehicle to High Wood

The High Wood perceived by today's visitor is of the same size and shape that would have confronted the eyes of a traveller prior to the First World War. Thus the visitor is gifted a large physical feature that greatly helps in understanding the layout of the battlefield and the nature of the fighting at this location. This tour is based on the use of the map 'Serie Bleue-Bray-sur-Somme' 2408 est' note that these maps do not overlap and also lack grid lines.

Commence the tour in Bapaume, a first day objective of the British Army's 1 July 1916 attack. Bapaume was an important supply and administration centre for the German Army. Knowing as we do that armies march on their stomachs, it is interesting to note that the Germans were engaged in mineral water bottling and baking bread on an industrial scale in Bapaume. Captured by Australians on 17 March 1917, the town was known to contain booby-traps – the Hotel de Ville subsequently blew up. Lost to the Germans on 24 March 1918, Bapaume was finally recaptured on 29 August by the New Zealand Division.

Leave Bapaume on the N17, travel approximately 3.1 miles (5 kilometres) then **turn left** on to D11 towards Villers-au-Flos. There is an interesting German War cemetery signposted from the village centre which contains 2,449 graves and also a memorial structure dedicated to the German XlV Korps. A British soldier was mortally wounded by shell splinters near Villers-au-Flos on 21 March 1918 dying on 30 March 1918 in the Duchess of Westminster's Hospital at Le Touquet; he is buried in the CWGC cemetery at Étaples. The soldier was Lieutenant Colonel Jasper Myers Richardson who at the age of 68 was the oldest British soldier to be killed in the First

Lieutenant Colonel Jasper Myers Richardson.

World War. Lieutenant Colonel Richardson was serving as an Agricultural Officer with V Corps. Born in Newcastle-on-Tyne he was a resident of Camden Square, Kensington in London.

Turn back towards Bapaume on N17 then take a **left turn** towards Ligny-Thilloy, carry straight on till D929 is reached, and **turn left** towards Albert. On the left side the Butte de Warlencourt will be seen, this 50ft high mound was a part of the Warlencourt Ridge defences denying Bapaume to the British. Pass through the village of Le Sars which stood on the German Third Line of defence in 1916, travel as far as the last house on the left, **turn left** here on to a track, look for some farm buildings and nearby is the remains of a German monument to their soldiers who died here during the Somme fighting. Return to D929 and carry on until a radio mast becomes visible on the left, **park on the right** where a memorial garden containing the remains of Pozières Windmill is located. The fine Tank Memorial, commemorating the brave men who first went to war in a motorised metal box, is situated on the opposite side of the road.

In the centre of Pozières, **turn left** on to D147 towards Contalmaison. At the junction with D20 **turn left** for Contalmaison. In Contalmaison centre **turn right** on to D147 towards Fricourt, down a slope on the outskirts of the village a grass track will be seen on **the right**, 250 yards along the track reveals the memorial (believed to be the smallest permanent memorial on the Somme) to Captain Francis Dodgson 8th

Captain Dodgson's Memorial, near Contalmaison.

Battalion Yorkshire Regiment who was killed 50m from this spot on 8 August 1916. The memorial originally stood 50m further away from Contalmaison; Captain Dodgson was buried at the original site. Against the wishes of the family, his remains were removed by CWGC to Serre Road No.2 Cemetery located on the D919 road south-west of the village of Serre, plot XXVIII, row K, Grave 8. The memorial is at its present position following the sale and division of land in 1962.

Return to the road and **turn right**. After a short drive Peak Wood Cemetery is reached which contains the grave of Captain Walshe (grave A15). Continue towards Fricourt, after a short distance the German Military cemetery will be reached on the left, this imposing site contains the remains of 17,026 German soldiers. The body of the famous flyer Manfred von Richthofen was interred here before being removed for burial in Germany. A little further along D147 a track will be seen on the right, **turn right** and park a short distance up the track. Fricourt New Military cemetery is reached by a short walk. The cemetery was started by the 10th West Yorkshire Regiment following their disastrous attack on 1 July 1916 when they buried their dead in the former no man's land;

the battalion suffered 710 casualties. A total of 210 soldiers are buried here, the cemetery as seen today being to the design of A.J.S. Hutton. One hundred yards south of the cemetery an area of large mounds can be seen, these are the remains of the Triple Tambour mines fired by the British to form a protective screen for the attacking troops of 21st Division. Unfortunately the Germans reached the crater rims before the attackers and wreaked havoc on the Yorkshire men.

Return to the vehicle and turn left onto D147, look for a track to the right about 200 yards beyond the German Cemetery, there is a wood here known to the British as 'Lozenge Wood', a quarter mile walk will lead to the 'Ferme du Bois' and a little further on where a cross track appears is the site of 'Fricourt Farm' the location of the advanced headquarters of Major General Barter's 47th (2nd London) Division during the 15 September attack. A buttress erected by the Germans to re-enforce a building can still be seen.

Imagine Barter's anguish, tied as he was to the telephone cable head, the only location in which he could receive orders direct from Corps or Army HQ. If for any reason he left his HQ he was effectively cut off, the closer to the active front that the general moved then the narrower

Contalmaison Church – Charles Fair noted that only three steps remained.

Three VC recipients: l-r, Serjeant Michael J. O'Leary, Corporal Edward Dwyer, Serjeant Douglas W. Belcher.

would be his view of the battle – that is if he could see anything of it at all. As for High Wood it stands 3¾ miles north-west of Fricourt Farm and was just one of Barter's responsibilities on that day. Barter's views regarding sending the new tanks into High Wood were disregarded but he would be held responsible for any failure; his position was not an enviable one.

Return to Contalmaison passing the church described by Charles Fair as consisting only of three steps. Go straight on to D20 in the direction of Longueval for 1¾ miles and look for a sign to Flat Iron Copse Cemetery **on the right**, this lane is known locally as 'Rue Santin', follow the lane to the cemetery. Lieutenant Colonel Hamilton is buried here in grave VII.1.2. The northern boundary wall of the cemetery is virtually the line of the jumping-off point for troops engaged in the 14 July battle for Bazentin Ridge. Edward Dwyer VC is buried here as are three sets of brothers: Tregaskis, Hardwidge and Philby.

Flat Iron Copse (Bois Santin) itself is situated opposite the cemetery gate; an Advanced Dressing Station (ADS) was located in the copse. Use of Global Positioning System (GPS) equipment has located earthworks in the interior of the copse that run at right angles to Rue Santin; there is also a flat area that would have been sheltered on two sides from incoming fire. There is a strong possibility that the flat area referred to is the site of the ADS. Should the traveller wish to proceed further beyond the cemetery on foot, the Welsh Dragon memorial situated in the infamous Death Valley can be visited.

Return to D20, and **turn right**, this road traverses the Bazentin Ridge and roughly follows the British front line captured on 14 July. At 0.7 miles a **right turn** to Bazentin-le-Grand will be reached, park safely on this road; not on D20. Cross D20 on foot to visit the only wayside crucifix known to have survived the war.

Wounded were collected here and given initial treatment prior to transfer to an ADS. Look along the road towards Longueval and you are seeing the area where the cavalry formed up to attack High Wood on 14 July. A track leaves the road just left of the Crucifix, a walk of 550 yards (at two paces to the yard) will bring the visitor to remains of Bazentin Mill with fine views of High Wood across ground devoid of cover. It was here that Frank Richards worked his signalling station and the German spy was apprehended. Retrace your steps to the Crucifix and walk towards Longueval, another track leaves the road on the **left**; this

Death Valley, 38th (Welsh) Division Memorial.

Death Valley Flat Iron Copse Cemetery.

Bazentin-le-Grand, Crucifix Corner).

track follows the route of Elgin Avenue and High Alley both of which formed the 'one-way' system to and from High Wood in this sector, Elgin Avenue being the 'up' route and High Alley the 'down'.

Order No.3 (Secret) for 140 Brigade declared:

Arrangements are being made for control posts who will detain all men coming back from the trenches who are not wearing a label signed by a medical officer, or runners wearing a blue strip around each cuff.

These posts were not places of fear for the straggler; on the contrary hot tea was provided together with something to eat and a sit down. The overwhelming majority of stragglers were quietly returned to their respective units none the worse for the experience. The Army recognised that soldiers who had been caught in the blast of exploding shells could have been thrown some distance and rendered unconscious or clawed their way out of burial by the soil thrown up by the exploding shells only to find that their comrades had disappeared. These men would have been suffering from shock and needed time to gather their wits. Pause awhile and imagine how it was here 100 years ago, by doing so, this landscape will begin to yield up its secrets.

Before leaving, note that the large farm visible from the crossroads is Bazentin-le-Grande Farm and the site of 140 Brigade HQ for the 15 September attack.

Proceed for ¾ mile along D20 in the direction of Longueval to arrive at Caterpillar Valley Cemetery, park on the right outside the cemetery. The cemetery grounds provide a grandstand view of the battlefield of 14 July to 15 September; Black Road, Wood Lane and High Wood are all clearly visible. The cemetery holds 5,539 burials, over 66 per cent of which are unidentified with many being victims of the High Wood fighting. The cemetery also holds the New Zealand Memorial to the Missing of the Somme as it was near this spot that the Kiwis launched their successful attack on 15 September. Many of the soldiers killed in the July attacks on Wood Lane and High Wood are buried here including Edwin Streatfield, grave V.C.4.

Continue on the D20 to the large crossroads in the centre of Longueval, **bear right**, then take a **left fork** at the Footballer's Memorial and park on the left for Delville Wood. After weeks of ferocious fighting,

New Zealand Memorial, located on the Switch Line, east of High Wood.

Delville Wood finally fell to the BEF. The wood can be explored on foot as in recent years the undergrowth has been cut back allowing the visitor to follow the trench lines and the course of the fighting. There is a very good museum in the wood itself which explains much of South Africa's role in the First World War. Nigel Cave's book *Delville Wood* is an excellent source of information on this most complex phase of the Battle of the Somme.

Turn left from the car park towards Ginchy. Park near the church in which two plaques record the deaths of Major Cedric Charles Dickens, grandson of the famous author and Lieutenant Charles Patrick Michael Irwin who was killed at Ginchy, aged 19. It was near Ginchy that due to the heavy fighting, the Germans were forced to re-locate their headquarters from Delville Wood. Harold Macmillan, who would go on to become Prime Minister of Great Britain, was wounded in this sector while serving in the Grenadier Guards. Prime Minister Asquith lost his son, Raymond, who was killed close by; he is buried in Guillemont Road cemetery.

Return to Longueval and **turn right on to the D147 for a short distance then take the left fork** where the D147 bears right, and follow this road to the obelisk that forms the New Zealand Memorial. Not only does this edifice commemorate that brave men came 'from the uttermost ends of the earth' to fight, it also stands, for all intents and purposes, on the Switch Line. The Kiwis advanced more than two miles and in doing so captured five miles of enemy-held trenches. Look across the old battlefield to High Wood's northern corner to follow the line of the Switch to gain an impression of the strength of the High Wood/Switch Line defences. The memorial was unveiled by a senior New Zealand legislator, Sir Francis Bell, in October 1922.

Return in the direction of Longueval for approximately 0.7 mile to a **right turn**; continue for approximately 300 yards until you reach an overgrown lane on the right. You are now at Wood Lane and the site of a German strongpoint that caused so many casualties to the British. Note that Wood Lane itself is a natural trench and look left to the crest of the adjacent field; attacking British troops were cut down here as they crested the skyline. The body density map below (CWGC) brings into sharp focus the severity of the fighting here and the high number of bodies recovered in later searches.

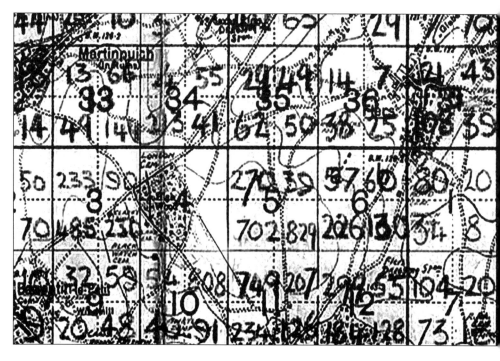

Cameron Highlanders and Black Watch Memorial.

Memorial Cairn, 9th Highland Light Infantry.

47th Division Memorial Garden, Martinpuich (Martin's Push).

Leave Wood Lane and proceed in the same direction to a 'T' junction with D107, **turn right** for 750 yards until you have reached **High Wood**. **Turn right** and proceed to the eastern corner of the wood; you are now following the line of Anderson trench. Note the memorials to the 20th Royal Fusiliers (Public Schools) Battalion and Black Watch and Cameron Highlanders before reaching the mine craters on the left. It is possible to park here and walk around the perimeter of the wood (see Walk One).

Martinpuich bunker.

Return to D107 and **turn right**, the 47th (London) Division Memorial will be seen on the right followed by that of the 9th Highland Light Infantry and on your **left** the London Cemetery and Extension (for full details, see Walk One). Follow D107 to the far end of High Wood and **turn left** towards Bazentin-le-Petit. This lane runs in part approximately on the line of Intermediate Trench and also contains the site of the German bunker where Charles Lander spent his horrific night. Look for the D73 in the direction of Pozières, note at the north end of Bazentin-le-Petit a small memorial to 'Nine Brave Men', all Royal Engineers who died here on the night of 29 July 1916. Proceed on the D73 to Pozières and the D929, **turn left** for Albert with its museum and eating places, or **turn right** for Bapaume.

A Walk around High Wood (walk one)

High Wood is the private property of the Mathon family; **do not enter the wood under any circumstances.** The owners have cared for the wood and the soldiers' remains contained within its bounds for a century, please allow it to remain so. With the aid of a French 'Serie Bleue' maps 2407 EST & 2408 EST, the visitor can easily locate High Wood standing as it does on the D107 road from Longueval to Martinpuich road (Martin's Push). A sign on the right shows 'Bois des Fourcaux/High Wood' **turn right** and proceed to the eastern corner of the wood and park well clear of the track. Be mindful that this is private land but in 39 years of visiting the writer has never had any issues with the farmer.

High Wood is closed but a path follows its four sides which can be walked in an hour's steady amble. From this eastern side, the maps can be used to locate the Switch Line where it exited the wood from this face. The New Zealand Memorial is visible to the right and you can also take in the massive advantage that possession of High Wood gave to the Germans. Look also for a gate which reveals the main ride through the

East side of High Wood, exit point of Switch Line. (Terry Carter)

Looking east to west in High Wood.

wood. Time and good management have healed the shattered remnants of High Wood that confronted the search parties of post 1918 who sought the remains of those listed as 'Missing Believed Killed' during the see-saw battles for the wood. The interior of the deciduous wood can be glimpsed from outside of the gate and it will quickly become apparent that High Wood guards her secrets well and does not give them up easily. Only the ride through the wood and its closely grown mature trees are revealed to the visitor, nothing can be seen to remind us of the immense battles that took place here so long ago during the summer of 1916.

Turn left on to the north face of the wood and look for the entry point of the Switch Line. Continue the circuit of the wood until it meets the D107, **turn left**; after a short distance, the London Cemetery and Extension is reached on the right. It is here that most of the friends and colleagues of Major Fair are buried, probably in a large shell hole where forty-seven men were buried between 18 – 21 September 1916; these graves are located to the left of the entrance gate. The cemetery holds 3,873 burials of which 3,114 are unidentified. Among those buried here are 165 British servicemen who were killed in this area during the Second World War.

North Side of High Wood; entry point of Switch Line. (Joyce Harrison)

Continuing the walk the visitor will find the monument to the 9th Highland Light Infantry (HLI). The simple but emotive cairn records the loss of 192 men of the 9th HLI who were killed in action near this spot on 15 September 1916. The cairn, which is constructed with 192 stones to the average height of a Highland soldier of the First World War, is the work of Mr and Mrs A. Aitkin and was unveiled in 1972.

The 47th (London) Division memorial is found a little further along D107. This is the second memorial on this site as the original which was erected in 1925 had to be replaced due to subsidence. Demolition took place circa 1994 with the replacement memorial being dedicated on 13 October 1996; the original cross and two of the cap stones were incorporated into the replacement. Some of the stones from the 1925 memorial live on, incorporated into the well-head in the garden of Ocean Villas Tea Room.

Moving in the same direction to the corner of the wood, a tree and plaque is located dedicated to the men of the 20th Royal Fusiliers (Public Schools) Battalion who fought here. **Turning left** and following the track on the line of Anderson Trench for approximately 250 yards, the site of Worcester Trench is reached. This is the location where tank D22 emerged from High Wood and opened fire on British troops. A little further on, the imposing Cameron Highlanders and Black Watch joint memorial is reached. The present memorial replaced the original which had been constructed from timber taken from the ruined villages on the battlefield.

Original Black Watch Memorial; south side of High Wood.

A short walk brings us to the mine craters located at spot height 158. The mines altered the landscape here forever and hundreds of soldiers from both sides died in the titanic struggles for the German strongpoint which occupied this site. Although High Wood is higher than the surrounding landscape, the mine craters are flooded, whereas the far larger and deeper surviving craters on the Somme are dry. The walk concludes with arrival at the east corner of the wood, the almost silent landscape only enforces the contrast with the visitor of today's experience with that of our ancestors who were here in 1916.

Walk from Quarry Cemetery to High Wood

The use of IGN map '2408 est' is recommended for this walk of approximately 5 miles. At the time of writing (April 2016) no outlets for food and drink can be found on this walk.

Note: in the absence of GPS devices, where distances are given in yards the standard two paces to the yard is a useful measure. This walk of approximately four hours duration covers the ground over which the British Army fought from 14 July to 15 September 1916. The visitor will walk in the footsteps of the troops who opened the way to High Wood, but nine weeks would elapse before the ejection of the German occupiers of the wood.

Take the D64 Montauban de Picardie road towards Guillemont **turning left** at the sign for Quarry Cemetery on the eastern outskirts of Montauban. The village of Montauban had fallen into British hands around noon on 1 July, the first fortified village to do so. Eye-witnesses reported that all of the 274 houses that made up the village had been destroyed beyond recognition. Where cellars could be accessed they were found to be full of dead German soldiers. Quarry Cemetery is reached 900 yards along the track which falls 25m from Montauban. The cemetery dates from 14 July 1916 when an advanced dressing station operated here during the battle and remained in use until February 1917 when the front moved further eastwards following the German Army's retreat to the Hindenburg Line.

Four small battlefield cemeteries, Briqueterie No.3, Caterpillar Wood No.2, Green Dump and Quarry Scottish Cemetery were closed and the remains reinterred here making a total of 756 burials, including fourteen German soldiers who were killed in the spring of 1918. The cemetery as seen today was designed by Sir Herbert Baker.

Montauban, Quarry Cemetery.

Before commencing the walk proper it is worth pausing at Quarry Cemetery to remember the men of the 18th and 30th Divisions who fought and won here on 1 July 1916. The divisions carried most of their objectives with a party of 17th Manchesters reaching a German artillery position known to the British as 'Triangle Point', located on the 133-metre contour, where they captured several guns. Also look northwards to see the landscape as British observers would have done on 1 July.

Commence the walk along the track towards Crucifix Corner, and look left to right for a panoramic view of the following features in the landscape: Caterpillar Wood, Mametz Wood, Marlborough Wood, Flat Iron Copse, Sabot Copse, Bazentin-le-Petit and Bazentin-le-Grand Woods, the Longueval Ridge, High Wood, Caterpillar Valley Cemetery, Delville Wood, Waterlot Farm, Trônes Wood, and Bernafay Wood. The price for possession of these heavily fortified hamlets, woods and valleys, would be the lives of thousands of men in the coming two months.

Quarry Cemetery lies in the topographical feature known to the British Army as 'Caterpillar Valley' a direct reference to the shape of the valley as it appeared on British Army trench maps. The French IGN map '2408 est' divides the valley with three separate names, Vallée du Bois, Vallée de Bapaume, and Vallée de Longueval. It was in this area that the finest sight that an infantryman ever sees was granted to British soldiers on 1 July 1916; that is 'the knap sacks of the enemy' who were streaming back towards Bazentin-le-Grand. This walk follows the men of the 14 July who successfully stormed the Bazentin Ridge and eventually, High Wood itself. Normally the British Army did not re-enforce failure as had occurred north-west of the Albert to Bapaume road on 1 July, whereas here south-east of the road, the success of the troops would be re-enforced. The British 3rd and 9th (Scottish) Division crossed Caterpillar Valley on 13 July meeting to establish themselves on the rising ground north of the cemetery.

Facing north from the cemetery, the land to the right is known as Vallée de Bapaume. There were never enough roads in the Somme battlefield area and even less undamaged routes for the reliable daily

Bazentin-le-Petit Quarry.

supply of the massive forces involved, without the further task of furnishing the extra supplies needed to mount an offensive. Much of the stores required for the 14 July attack and subsequent operations to secure High Wood were sent via Caterpillar Valley and Happy Valley (later Death Valley) which was, and still is, a wide flat-bottomed route pointing straight towards the front lines. The only viable alternative route to the front for transport was the road we shall encounter on this walk which emerges on to the D20 road at Bazentin-le-Grand. Spare a moment to think of the gunners who had to live here in Caterpillar Valley as the British poured ever more artillery pieces into the valley from where, the Bazentins, Martinpuich, High Wood, Longueval, and Delville Wood were now within range. The crash and roar of the guns was incessant and at night the valley was lit up by the muzzle flash of the guns. For the unlucky occupants of the valley, sleep was impossible, added to which the German former occupants swept the area several times day and night with artillery ensuring that dismemberment, death and total destruction could come crashing out of the sky at any moment.

Remember also the horses, who did not volunteer. When on 22 July several hundred of our equine comrades came under shell fire, to save as many of the animals as possible they were cut loose. Deciding that they had had enough of the war, the horses stampeded rearwards out of Caterpillar Valley; note that the horses had enough sense not to run in the opposite direction towards the front lines. By a miracle, the vast majority of the horses survived the day.

The artillery concentration in Caterpillar Valley caused apprehension in the British High Command that the enemy might venture forth from the unsecured area of Longueval and capture or destroy a significant part of Fourth Army's artillery. Concern was also rising regarding the daily consumption of gun ammunition. GHQ had contacted Fourth Army as early as 2 July to remind staffs that the daily supply of 18-pounder ammunition was 'only' 56,000 rounds. For the 6-inch guns, only 5,000 rounds per day could be spared. Spread over the whole eighteen miles of Fourth Army front 3,111, 18-pounder shells were available per mile each day.

Imagine this place 100 years ago, the noise alone cannot be replicated – 'the smaller the gun the bigger the bang'. As the 18-pounders crashed out to the accompaniment of the deeper roar of the heavy guns, the shattering explosions of incoming shells caused huge clouds of dust and

Disused path, north of Quarry Cemetery.

smoke accompanied by hails of whirling, deadly shards of metal. Thirst also became a problem for the troops as all supplies had to be man-carried forward in any receptacle that came to hand and as such was frequently lost leaving men to cope as best they could with the summer heat, dust, and smoke. All this drama of life and death was played out here where you are standing: *Listen awhile, you will hear them still.*

Proceed North for 220 yards to spot height 108 where the line of a former track can be seen. This track climbed quickly to a height of 139m before gently descending to 137m where it joined the D20 road opposite Thistle Dump Cemetery. Ignore the former track and take the **left fork**. The track clears Caterpillar Valley and emerges onto the 'Plaine of Saint Anne'. We have now crossed the British front line of 14 July in the general direction taken by 3rd and 9th Divisions. The German front line was located approximately 100 yards north from here. Imagine yourself as an observer standing here at 03.25am on 14 July 1916, thousands of British troops were storming forward, 'leaning on the barrage', to burst into the enemy's positions before he had time to react.

The Scots of 26 and 27 brigades reached Delville Wood without meeting opposition, 3rd Division with 8 and 9 brigades were held up by uncut wire in front of Bazentin-le-Grand. The situation was resolved by men of the 2nd Royal Scots who faced left and proceeded to oust the enemy by the use of hand grenades. With the enemy now subdued, 8 and 9 brigades pressed forward and, despite heavy machine-gun fire, stormed and captured Bazentin-le-Grand which was later used as HQ by 140 Brigade for 15 September attack.

Follow the track in the footsteps of the Tommies to **spot height 127** on the Bazentin Ridge which became the British front line on what is now the **D20 road at Crucifix Corner**. It would have been from here that our imaginary observer witnessed the seemingly impossible: fortified villages had been captured and state-of-the-art trench systems ruptured – the way to High Wood was open. It was a remarkable feat of arms by soldiers who had been deemed incapable of such a manoeuvre by their own and allied high commands.

It was along this D20 road that the 7th Dragoon Guards and 20th Deccan Horse assembled for their much-delayed charge against High Wood. **Thistle Dump Cemetery** is located approximately 660 yards to the right. Caterpillar Valley Cemetery can be reached ¾ mile to the right.

By turning right at the Crucifix a short walk leads to a substantial track on the left that leads north-east towards High Wood which lies ¾ of a mile away. This track existed in 1916 and allows the explorer to follow the routes of High Alley and Elgin Alley. Both were communication trenches that ran almost parallel to the track, High Alley was to the left and Elgin Alley to the right of the track when facing High Wood. These trenches formed the main routes up to High Wood for 140 Brigade, rising from 127 to 152 metres at the south-west corner of High Wood. We are also in the area where posts were established to detain unauthorised people from leaving the battle area. The lower part of High Alley was used as a return route for the 'runners' of 104 and 141 brigades.

On the night of 13/14 September 1916, the D Company tanks allotted to 47th Division had moved up as far as Lozenge Wood just north of Fricourt on what is now the D147 and shown on the modern map as Bois de la Ferme, there to wait for nightfall before proceeding to their assembly area at the head of Flat Iron Valley at S14a 3.4. The three tanks (later joined by a fourth machine, C23) then travelled parallel to the D20 towards the Crucifix before making a turn half left to join the track to High Wood. If ever it can truly be said that we walk in the footsteps of history, then this humble track allows us to do just that. Here men in their thousands and clanking metal monsters set out on a journey to a very uncertain future.

Proceeding along the track and facing High Wood pause and look left; approximately 300 yards distant is the line of Argyll Trench that ran from just north of the Windmill to a junction with Bedford Street, approximately 500 yards south-west of High Wood. Argyle Trench served as the 'up route' for 141 Brigade on 15 September.

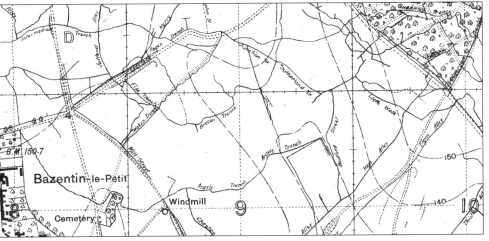

Argyle Trench.

Elgin Alley joined what is now the D107 road at **spot height 152,** approximately 50 yards to the right of the corner of High Wood as our track from the Crucifix emerges. This part of the D107 is the site of 'Black Road' that faces the parallel trench systems that featured in the battles for Wood Lane which still lies some 340 yards straight ahead. The boundary of 47th and the New Zealand Divisions was located a further 140 yards along D107 in the direction of Longueval. High Alley reached the D107 just a few yards to the right of where the 47th (2nd London) Division Memorial now stands; a fitting location indeed.

Directly opposite where the track from Crucifix Corner meets D20 the line of Anderson Trench follows the left of the track up the side of

High Wood towards the mine craters. Follow Anderson Trench for 250 yards to the junction with Worcester Trench which entered from the right. On 15 September, 140 Brigade, 7th London (City of London) Rifles attacked from here on a line that crossed Wood Lane to a point approximately 350 yards west. Also with 140 Brigade, 15th London (Civil Service) Rifles attacked on a line from the junction of Anderson and Worcester trenches into High Wood via Queens Trench to Sap 4, from where,141 Brigade took over responsibility for a line from Sap 4 to a point on what is now the D107 opposite where the long north wall of London Cemetery now stands. The 17th London (Poplar & Stepney) Rifles were actually in High Wood from Sap 4 to the road from where 18th London (London Irish) Rifles attacked from Fife Trench which ran south-west parallel to the north wall of London Cemetery before a junction which turned north-west facing High Wood.

For the battlefield walker, the D107 and London Cemetery serve as reference points to aid understanding of the 15 September attack; by standing with the back to the cemetery and doing the same along the road to where our track emerged opposite Anderson Trench, the walker is observing the direction of the attack and the ground from which the Londoners launched themselves against the High Wood defences. Also of importance to note, four of the tanks that went into action on the first

Junction of Anderson and Worcester Trenches; South Side of High Wood. (Terry Carter)

day of their battlefield deployment entered High Wood from this road between the cemetery and the corner of High Wood at Anderson Trench, the tanks used here being D13, D21, D22, C23.

From here it is recommended that the walker refers to 'A Walk Around High Wood' where full details of the landscape and history can be found.

High Wood to Crucifix Corner via Bazentin-le-Petit

For the return route it is recommended to follow the lane opposite the **north-west corner** of High Wood in the direction of **Bazenti–le-Petit** along which the line of Intermediate Trench and the Elbow can be traced using the trench maps. To the left is the area of the 'Grande Vallée', note the numerous closely-spaced contour lines on the modern map; using the spot heights and contour lines creates a useful picture of the problems facing the BEF during the High Wood fighting. Before turning **left at spot Height 147**, walkers may wish to extend their exploration by going straight ahead for a short distance where located in some bushes on the left of the track, is the private memorial to Captain Houston Stewart Hamilton Wallace. Captain Wallace was killed in action north-east of his memorial on 22 July 1916; he is officially commemorated on the Thiepval Memorial.

Return to **spot height 147** and turn **right** onto the track known as Mill Street in 1916. After 250 yards, the line of Waters Trench will be crossed. This trench linked with a track that ran from the quarry in Bazentin-le-Petit to Mill Street; Waters Street then ran on to a point on the lane from High Wood to Bazentin-le-Petit joining the lane near the Elbow. Looking south-west from this spot, 200 yards distant a clump of trees will be observed; these mark the site of the quarry used by 149 Brigade as headquarters for the 15 September attack. The quarry was also used by the Royal Army Medical Corps and Robert Graves was brought for preliminary treatment following his wounding. The site is now the location of CWGC Bazentin-le-Petit Communal Cemetery Extension.

A further 300 yards leads to the point where Argyll Trench crossed Mill Street, having originated at the above mentioned quarry before heading north-east across the Grande Vallée. John Miller VC died roughly 450 yards north-east of the quarry which coincides with a point on Waters Street. A short distance further along Mill Street a large

Wallace memorial.

overgrown mound will be seen on the right. This is the site of Frank Richard's windmill. Pause here and think of Frank, his comrades, the Rat, and the German spy all caught up in the inferno of the Somme.

On reaching Crucifix Corner retrace your steps to Quarry Cemetery; take the time to observe the landscape as the Germans would have known it as you are walking head on into the British line of advance of 14 July 1916. Perhaps the ghosts of those Germans who fled Montauban on 1 July are passing you as you amble through this historic landscape?

Extract from the *Birmingham Daily Gazette* 14 October 1924
Courtesy of British Newspaper Archive

THE FADING BATTLE-FRONT
II – ON THE SOMME
By 'A Correspondent'

In High Wood

On this ground there was still standing a German pill-box – whether it dated from 1916 or 1918 I do not know, but there were bullet and shell splashes all over it. It had been most cleverly built, the western side was made by filling boilers, evidently part of the sugar-refining plant, with concrete, and against this bulwark was constructed a miniature fort of reinforced concrete. The roof was several feet thick, and would stand a direct hit from any shell up to 6in.

I now turned right-handed through the oval-shaped village of Martinpuich to the historic High Wood. This wood has no large trees living, and the dead trunks are surrounded with impenetrable undergrowth. Finding one of the old rides re-opened, I walked through to the eastern edge.

An uncanny silence reigned over this tangled mass of woodland, where we had thousands of casualties in two months' close fighting and, even in the bright noon sunlight, it was no place to linger in.

I went down the far side over Switch Trench to the point where Cork Alley ran into the wood; in this corner there were a number of shell holes filled with water, and the soil had been recently disturbed, probably by parties looking for solitary graves. Standing here, among the blasted trees and the shell holes in the freshly-turned ground, one almost expected to hear the slam of 18-pounders about the Bazentins, and the thud of 'heavies' in Caterpillar Valley. Near here is a memorial stone to two Highland Battalions, the Black Watch and the 1st Cameron Highlanders.

The road leading southwards brought me to Longueval; on the left of the road a farmer was ploughing a field in front of the site of the trench called Wood-lane, and his plough was turning up relics of the epic fighting that took place on this ground.

Longueval is in course of reconstruction, and turning left in the centre of the village, I entered Delville Wood, going along the drive that the Scots nicknamed Princes-street. In the middle of the wood South Africa is erecting a very fine memorial to commemorate the bitter fighting of her men here in 1916.

I climbed up this memorial and had a bird's-eye view of the core of the Somme Battlefields – the undergrowth not so thick and tall as that of High Wood, much of it being blackberry bushes; the new roofs of Lesboeufs and Morval topped the crest of stubble fields to the east. Ginchy and Guillemont were again proper villages with houses and gardens, and a large factory was rising in the neighbourhood.

(Spelling and punctuation as per original article)

In High Wood.

On this ground there was still standing a German pill-box—whether it dated from 1916 or 1918 I do not know, but there were bullet and shell splashes all over it. It had been most cleverly built, the western side was made by filling boilers, evidently part of the sugar-refining plant, with concrete, and against this bulwark was constructed a miniature fort of reinforced concrete. The roof was several feet thick, and would stand a direct hit from any shell up to 6in.

I now turned right-handed through the oval-shaped village of Martinpuich to the historic High Wood. This wood has no large trees living, and the dead trunks are surrounded with impenetrable undergrowth. Finding one of the old rides re-opened, I walked through to the eastern edge.

An uncanny silence reigned over this tangled mass of woodland, where we had thousands of casualties in two months' close fighting and, even in the bright noon sunlight, it was no place to linger in.

I went down the far side over Switch Trench to the point where Cork Alley ran into the wood; in this corner there were a number of shell holes filled with water, and the soil had been recently disturbed, probably by parties looking for solitary graves. Standing here, among the blasted trees and the shell-holes in the freshly-turned ground, one almost expected to hear the slam of 18-pounders about the Bazentins, and the thud of "heavies" in Caterpillar Valley. Near here is a memorial stone to two Highland battalions, the Black Watch and the 1st Cameron Highlanders.

I saw many British cemeteries during the day, and the remarks I made about the beautiful condition of those in the Ypres salient are equally applicable to the cemeteries on the Somme.

Albert itself is in the throes of reconstruction. Many of the original house sites, cleared of debris, have not yet had any buildings constructed on them, and under these sites I could see the cellars used by us and the Germans as shelters. These cellars had been connected from house to house by rough gaps in the partition walls.

The cathedral is still a heap of ruins, and a temporary church has been built near the north-east corner. A replica of the famous golden figure of the Virgin, which, struck by a shell in January, 1915, for three and a half years hung at right angles to the old tower, glitters on the new church roof.

In this town, as in the rest of France and Belgium, the people work hard for many hours a day and often on Sundays; their one aim is to restore their country to what it was before the flames of war smashed the houses, destroyed the trees and vegetation, and devastated the soil. They are succeeding admirably in their efforts, and the result is an object lesson in what a nation can achieve if everybody really works with a will.

AFTER BIG GAME.

"THE HIGH GRASS TRAIL." By Frank Saville. Illustrated. (Witherby. 16s.)

When the grass is high in Nyassaland and Northern Rhodesia, the sportsman has to "feel" for game rather than stalk it. Mr. Saville's account of a

Selective Bibliography

Anon, *Military Mining 1914-1918*, Naval & Military Press

Bull, Dr Stephen, *An Officer's Manual of the Western Front*, compiled from Army Printing and Stationery Services publications 1914-1918

Boraston, J.H., *Sir Douglas Haig's Despatches*, Dent, 1919

Brown, Malcolm, *The Imperial War Museum Book of the Somme*, Macmillan, 1997

Carrington, Charles, *Soldiers From the War Returning*, Hutchinson, 1965

Carter, Terry, *Birmingham Pals*, Pen & Sword, 1997

Chasseaud, Peter, *Artillery's Astrologers*, Mapbooks, 1999

Crutchley, C.E., *Machine Gunners 1914-1918*, Bailey Bros. & Swinfen, 1975

Cuttle, Barry, *148 Days on the Somme*, GMS Enterprises, 2000

Duffy, Christopher, *Through German Eyes*, Weidenfeld & Nicolson, 2006

Dunn, Captain J., *The War the Infantry Knew*, King, 1938

Edmunds, Sir James, *Official History of the Great War, Vol. 2, Land Operations France and Belgium 1916*, Imperial War Museum, 1932

Farr, Don, *The Silent General*, Helion, 2007

Farrar-Hockley, Sir A.H. *The Somme*, Batsford, 1964

Fischer, Fritz, *Germany's Aim in the First World War*, W.W. Norton, New York, 1967

Foulkes, Major General C.H., *Gas – The Story of the Special Brigade*, Blackwood, 1936

Gliddon, Gerald, *The Battle of the Somme, a Topographical History*, Sutton, 1998

Gliddon, Gerald, *VCs of World War One: The Somme*, Gliddon Books, 1991

Glubb, John, *Into Battle – A Soldier's Diary of the Great War*, Cassell, 1978

Greive & Newman, *Tunnellers: the Story of the Tunnelling Companies, Royal Engineers*, Jenkins, 1936

Griffith, Paddy, *The Great War on the Western Front*, Pen & Sword, 2008

Griffith, Paddy, *Battle Tactics of the Western Front: The British Army's Art of Attack 1916-1918*, Yale University Press, 1994

Harrison, Michael, *Lander's War*, Menin House, 2010

Holmes, Richard, *Tommy: The British Soldier on the Western Front 1914-1918*, Harper Collins, 2004

Hutchinson, Lieutenant Colonel, *Machine Guns*, Naval & Military Press, 2004

James, Captain E.A., *A Record of the Battles and Engagements of the British Armies in France and Flanders 1914-1918*, The London Stamp Exchange, 1990 edition 1924 original

Knight, Gill, *Civil Service Rifles in the Great War*, Pen & Sword, 2005

Lewis-Stemple, John, *Six Weeks*, Orion, 2011

Luttwak, E.W., *Strategy: The Logic of Peace and War*, Harvard College, 2003

Masefield, John, *The Battle of the Somme*, 1919 [reprint by Forgotten Books 2015]

McCarthy, Chris, *The Somme: the Day By Day Account*, Brockhampton Press, 1998

Norman, Terry, *The Hell They Called High Wood*, Kimber, 1984

Philpott, William, *Bloody Victory*, Little, Brown, 2009

Pidgeon, Trevor, *The Tanks At Flers*, Fairmile, 1995

Pidgeon, Trevor, *Tanks on the Somme*, Pen & Sword, 2010

Prior & Wilson, *Command on the Western Front: The Military Career of Sir Henry Rawlinson 1914-1918*, Pen & Sword 2004

Reed, Paul, *Walking the Somme*, Leo Cooper 1997

Reid, Walter, *Douglas Haig, Architect of Victory*, Birlinn, 2009

Richards, Frank, *Old Soldiers Never Die*, Faber & Faber, 1933

Sheffield, Gary, *The Somme*, Cassell, 2004

Sheldon, Jack, *The German Army on the Somme 1914-1916*, Pen & Sword, 2005

Stewart, Cameron, *A Very Unimportant Officer*, Hodder, 2009

Sun Tzu, *The Art of War*, Oxford University Press, 1963

Swinton, Sir Ernest, *Twenty Years After: The Battlefields of 1914-1918: Then & Now*, Newnes, 1938

Terraine, John, *The Smoke and the Fire: The Myths and anti myths of War 1861-1945*, Leo Cooper, 1992

Terraine, John, *Business In Great Waters*, Leo Cooper, 1989

Veitch, Major E.H., *8th Battalion, The Durham Light Infantry 1793-1926*, Veitch, 1926

Westlake, Ray, *Tracing British Battalions on the Somme*, Pen & Sword, 2009

Wright, Patrick, *Tank*, Faber & Faber, 2000

Wyrall, Everard, *The 50th Division 1914-1919*, Naval & Military Press, reprint of 1939

Selective Index

·